JUDGES AND RUTH

THE IGNATIUS CATHOLIC STUDY BIBLE

REVISED STANDARD VERSION
SECOND CATHOLIC EDITION

JUDGES AND RUTH

With Introduction, Commentary, and Notes

by

Scott Hahn and Curtis Mitch

with

Michael Barber

and

with Study Questions by

Dennis Walters

IGNATIUS PRESS SAN FRANCISCO

Published with ecclesiastical approval

Original RSV Bible text:
Revised Standard Version, Catholic Edition
Imprimatur: + Gordon Joseph Gray
Archbishop of Saint Andrews and Edinburgh
Epiphany, 1966
Imprimatur: + Peter W. Bartholome, D.D.
Bishop of St. Cloud, Minnesota
May 11, 1966

Introduction, commentaries, and notes:
Nihil Obstat: Dr. Ruth Ohm Sutherland, Ph.D., M.T.S.
Imprimatur: + The Most Reverend Salvatore Cordileone
Archbishop of San Francisco
February 20, 2015

Second Catholic Edition approved by the
National Council of the Churches of Christ in the USA

Cover art: Francesco Fontebasso (1707–1769)
Gideon's Sacrifice (detail)

Cover designer: Riz Boncan Marsella

Published by Ignatius Press in 2015

ISBN 978-1-58617-912-0
Printed in the United States of America ♾

CONTENTS

INTRODUCTION TO THE IGNATIUS STUDY BIBLE

by Scott Hahn, Ph.D.

You are approaching the "word of God". This is the title Christians most commonly give to the Bible, and the expression is rich in meaning. It is also the title given to the Second Person of the Blessed Trinity, God the Son. For Jesus Christ became flesh for our salvation, and "the name by which he is called is The Word of God" (Rev 19:13; cf. Jn 1:14).

The word of God is Scripture. The Word of God is Jesus. This close association between God's *written* word and his *eternal* Word is intentional and has been the custom of the Church since the first generation. "All Sacred Scripture is but one book, and this one book is Christ, 'because all divine Scripture speaks of Christ, and all divine Scripture is fulfilled in Christ'[1]" (CCC 134). This does not mean that the Scriptures are divine in the same way that Jesus is divine. They are, rather, divinely inspired and, as such, are unique in world literature, just as the Incarnation of the eternal Word is unique in human history.

Yet we can say that the inspired word resembles the incarnate Word in several important ways. Jesus Christ is the Word of God incarnate. In his humanity, he is like us in all things, except for sin. As a work of man, the Bible is like any other book, except without error. Both Christ and Scripture, says the Second Vatican Council, are given "for the sake of our salvation" (*Dei Verbum* 11), and both give us God's definitive revelation of himself. We cannot, therefore, conceive of one without the other: the Bible without Jesus, or Jesus without the Bible. Each is the interpretive key to the other. And because Christ is the subject of all the Scriptures, St. Jerome insists, "Ignorance of the Scriptures is ignorance of Christ"[2] (CCC 133).

When we approach the Bible, then, we approach Jesus, the Word of God; and in order to encounter Jesus, we must approach him in a prayerful study of the inspired word of God, the Sacred Scriptures.

Inspiration and Inerrancy The Catholic Church makes mighty claims for the Bible, and our acceptance of those claims is essential if we are to read the Scriptures and apply them to our lives as the Church intends. So it is not enough merely to nod at words like "inspired", "unique", or "inerrant". We have to understand what the Church means by these

terms, and we have to make that understanding our own. After all, what we believe about the Bible will inevitably influence the way we read the Bible. The way we read the Bible, in turn, will determine what we "get out" of its sacred pages.

These principles hold true no matter what we read: a news report, a search warrant, an advertisement, a paycheck, a doctor's prescription, an eviction notice. How (or whether) we read these things depends largely upon our preconceived notions about the reliability and authority of their sources—and the potential they have for affecting our lives. In some cases, to misunderstand a document's authority can lead to dire consequences. In others, it can keep us from enjoying rewards that are rightfully ours. In the case of the Bible, both the rewards and the consequences involved take on an ultimate value.

What does the Church mean, then, when she affirms the words of St. Paul: "All Scripture is inspired by God" (2 Tim 3:16)? Since the term "inspired" in this passage could be translated "God-breathed", it follows that God breathed forth his word in the Scriptures as you and I breathe forth air when we speak. This means that God is the primary author of the Bible. He certainly employed human authors in this task as well, but he did not merely assist them while they wrote or subsequently approve what they had written. God the Holy Spirit is the *principal* author of Scripture, while the human writers are *instrumental* authors. These human authors freely wrote everything, and only those things, that God wanted: the word of God in the very words of God. This miracle of dual authorship extends to the whole of Scripture, and to every one of its parts, so that whatever the human authors affirm, God likewise affirms through their words.

The principle of biblical inerrancy follows logically from this principle of divine authorship. After all, God cannot lie, and he cannot make mistakes. Since the Bible is divinely inspired, it must be without error in everything that its divine and human authors affirm to be true. This means that biblical inerrancy is a mystery even broader in scope than infallibility, which guarantees for us that the Church will always teach the truth concerning faith and morals. Of course the mantle of inerrancy likewise covers faith and morals, but it extends even farther to ensure that all the facts and events of salvation history are accurately presented for us in the Scriptures. Inerrancy is our guarantee that the

[1] Hugh of St. Victor, *De arca Noe* 2, 8: PL 176, 642: cf. ibid. 2, 9: PL 176, 642–43.
[2] *DV* 25; cf. Phil 3:8 and St. Jerome, *Commentariorum Isaiam libri xviii*, prol.: PL 24, 17b.

words and deeds of God found in the Bible are unified and true, declaring with one voice the wonders of his saving love.

The guarantee of inerrancy does not mean, however, that the Bible is an all-purpose encyclopedia of information covering every field of study. The Bible is not, for example, a textbook in the empirical sciences, and it should not be treated as one. When biblical authors relate facts of the natural order, we can be sure they are speaking in a purely descriptive and "phenomenological" way, according to the way things appeared to their senses.

Biblical Authority Implicit in these doctrines is God's desire to make himself known to the world and to enter a loving relationship with every man, woman, and child he has created. God gave us the Scriptures not just to inform or motivate us; more than anything he wants to save us. This higher purpose underlies every page of the Bible, indeed every word of it.

In order to reveal himself, God used what theologians call "accommodation". Sometimes the Lord stoops down to communicate by "condescension"— that is, he speaks as humans speak, as if he had the same passions and weakness that we do (for example, God says he was "sorry" that he made man in Genesis 6:6). Other times he communicates by "elevation"—that is, by endowing human words with divine power (for example, through the Prophets). The numerous examples of divine accommodation in the Bible are an expression of God's wise and fatherly ways. For a sensitive father can speak with his children either by condescension, as in baby talk, or by elevation, by bringing a child's understanding up to a more mature level.

God's word is thus saving, fatherly, and personal. Because it speaks directly to us, we must never be indifferent to its content; after all, the word of God is at once the object, cause, and support of our faith. It is, in fact, a test of our faith, since we see in the Scriptures only what faith disposes us to see. If we believe what the Church believes, we will see in Scripture the saving, inerrant, and divinely authored revelation of the Father. If we believe otherwise, we see another book altogether.

This test applies not only to rank-and-file believers but also to the Church's theologians and hierarchy, and even the Magisterium. Vatican II has stressed in recent times that Scripture must be "the very soul of sacred theology" (*Dei Verbum* 24). As Joseph Cardinal Ratzinger, Pope Benedict XVI echoed this powerful teaching with his own, insisting that, "The *normative theologians* are the authors of Holy Scripture" (emphasis added). He reminded us that Scripture and the Church's dogmatic teaching are tied tightly together, to the point of being inseparable: "Dogma is by definition nothing other than an interpretation of Scripture." The defined dogmas of our faith, then, encapsulate the Church's infallible interpretation of Scripture, and theology is a further reflection upon that work.

The Senses of Scripture Because the Bible has both divine and human authors, we are required to master a different sort of reading than we are used to. First, we must read Scripture according to its *literal* sense, as we read any other human literature. At this initial stage, we strive to discover the meaning of the words and expressions used by the biblical writers as they were understood in their original setting and by their original recipients. This means, among other things, that we do not interpret everything we read "literalistically", as though Scripture never speaks in a figurative or symbolic way (it often does!). Rather, we read it according to the rules that govern its different literary forms of writing, depending on whether we are reading a narrative, a poem, a letter, a parable, or an apocalyptic vision. The Church calls us to read the divine books in this way to ensure that we understand what the human authors were laboring to explain to God's people.

The literal sense, however, is not the only sense of Scripture, since we interpret its sacred pages according to the *spiritual* senses as well. In this way, we search out what the Holy Spirit is trying to tell us, beyond even what the human authors have consciously asserted. Whereas the literal sense of Scripture describes a historical reality—a fact, precept, or event—the spiritual senses disclose deeper mysteries revealed through the historical realities. What the soul is to the body, the spiritual senses are to the literal. You can distinguish them; but if you try to separate them, death immediately follows. St. Paul was the first to insist upon this and warn of its consequences: "God ... has qualified us to be ministers of a new covenant, not in a written code but in the Spirit; for the written code kills, but the Spirit gives life" (2 Cor 3:5–6).

Catholic tradition recognizes three spiritual senses that stand upon the foundation of the literal sense of Scripture (see CCC 115). (**1**) The first is the *allegorical* sense, which unveils the spiritual and prophetic meaning of biblical history. Allegorical interpretations thus reveal how persons, events, and institutions of Scripture can point beyond themselves toward greater mysteries yet to come (OT) or display the fruits of mysteries already revealed (NT). Christians have often read the Old Testament in this way to discover how the mystery of Christ in the New Covenant was once hidden in the Old and how the full significance of the Old Covenant was finally made manifest in the New. Allegorical significance is likewise latent in the New Testament, especially in the life and deeds of Jesus recorded in the Gospels. Because Christ is the Head of the Church and the source of her spiritual life, what was accomplished in Christ the Head during his earthly life prefigures what he continually produces in his members through grace. The allegorical sense builds up the virtue of faith. **(2)** The second is the *tropological* or *moral* sense, which reveals how the actions of God's people in the Old Testament and the life of Jesus in the New Testament prompt us to form virtuous habits in our own lives. It therefore draws from Scripture warnings against sin and vice as well as inspirations to pursue holiness and purity. The moral sense is intended to build up the virtue of charity. **(3)** The third is the *anagogical* sense, which points upward to heavenly glory. It shows us how countless events in the Bible prefigure our final union with God in eternity and how things that are "seen" on earth are figures of things "unseen" in heaven. Because the anagogical sense leads us to contemplate our destiny, it is meant to build up the virtue of hope. Together with the literal sense, then, these spiritual senses draw out the fullness of what God wants to give us through his Word and as such comprise what ancient tradition has called the "full sense" of Sacred Scripture.

All of this means that the deeds and events of the Bible are charged with meaning beyond what is immediately apparent to the reader. In essence, that meaning is Jesus Christ and the salvation he died to give us. This is especially true of the books of the New Testament, which proclaim Jesus explicitly; but it is also true of the Old Testament, which speaks of Jesus in more hidden and symbolic ways. The human authors of the Old Testament told us as much as they were able, but they could not clearly discern the shape of all future events standing at such a distance. It is the Bible's divine Author, the Holy Spirit, who could and did foretell the saving work of Christ, from the first page of the Book of Genesis onward.

The New Testament did not, therefore, abolish the Old. Rather, the New fulfilled the Old, and in doing so, it lifted the veil that kept hidden the face of the Lord's bride. Once the veil is removed, we suddenly see the world of the Old Covenant charged with grandeur. Water, fire, clouds, gardens, trees, hills, doves, lambs—all of these things are memorable details in the history and poetry of Israel. But now, seen in the light of Jesus Christ, they are much more. For the Christian with eyes to see, water symbolizes the saving power of Baptism; fire, the Holy Spirit; the spotless lamb, Christ crucified; Jerusalem, the city of heavenly glory.

The spiritual reading of Scripture is nothing new. Indeed, the very first Christians read the Bible this way. St. Paul describes Adam as a "type" that prefigured Jesus Christ (Rom 5:14). A "type" is a real person, place, thing, or event in the Old Testament that foreshadows something greater in the New. From this term we get the word "typology", referring to the study of how the Old Testament prefigures Christ (CCC 128–30). Elsewhere St. Paul draws deeper meanings out of the story of Abraham's sons, declaring, "This is an allegory" (Gal 4:24). He is not suggesting that these events of the distant past never really happened; he is saying that the events both happened *and* signified something more glorious yet to come.

The New Testament later describes the Tabernacle of ancient Israel as "a copy and shadow of the heavenly sanctuary" (Heb 8:5) and the Mosaic Law as a "shadow of the good things to come" (Heb 10:1). St. Peter, in turn, notes that Noah and his family were "saved through water" in a way that "corresponds" to sacramental Baptism, which "now saves you" (1 Pet 3:20–21). It is interesting to note that the expression translated as "corresponds" in this verse is a Greek term that denotes the fulfillment or counterpart of an ancient "type".

We need not look to the apostles, however, to justify a spiritual reading of the Bible. After all, Jesus himself read the Old Testament this way. He referred to Jonah (Mt 12:39), Solomon (Mt 12:42), the Temple (Jn 2:19), and the brazen serpent (Jn 3:14) as "signs" that pointed forward to him. We see in Luke's Gospel, as Christ comforted the disciples on the road to Emmaus, that "beginning with Moses and all the prophets, he interpreted to them in all the Scriptures the things concerning himself" (Lk 24:27). It was precisely this extensive spiritual interpretation of the Old Testament that made such an impact on these once-discouraged travelers, causing their hearts to "burn" within them (Lk 24:32).

Criteria for Biblical Interpretation We, too, must learn to discern the "full sense" of Scripture as it includes both the literal and spiritual senses together. Still, this does not mean we should "read into" the Bible meanings that are not really there. Spiritual exegesis is not an unrestrained flight of the imagination. Rather, it is a sacred science that proceeds according to certain principles and stands accountable to sacred tradition, the Magisterium, and the wider community of biblical interpreters (both living and deceased).

In searching out the full sense of a text, we should always avoid the extreme tendency to "over-spiritualize" in a way that minimizes or denies the Bible's literal truth. St. Thomas Aquinas was well aware of this danger and asserted that "all other senses of Sacred Scripture are based on the literal" (*STh* I, 1, 10, *ad* 1, quoted in CCC 116). On the other hand, we should never confine the meaning of a text to the literal, intended sense of its human author, as if the divine Author did not intend the passage to be read in the light of Christ's coming.

Fortunately the Church has given us guidelines in our study of Scripture. The unique character and divine authorship of the Bible call us to read it "in the Spirit" (*Dei Verbum* 12). Vatican II outlines this teaching in a practical way by directing us to read the Scriptures according to three specific criteria:

1. We must "[b]e especially attentive 'to the content and unity of the whole Scripture'" (CCC 112).

9

2. We must "[r]ead the Scripture within 'the living Tradition of the whole Church'" (CCC 113).

3. We must "[b]e attentive to the analogy of faith" (CCC 114; cf. Rom 12:6).

These criteria protect us from many of the dangers that ensnare readers of the Bible, from the newest inquirer to the most prestigious scholar. Reading Scripture out of context is one such pitfall, and probably the one most difficult to avoid. A memorable cartoon from the 1950s shows a young man poring over the pages of the Bible. He says to his sister: "Don't bother me now; I'm trying to find a Scripture verse to back up one of my preconceived notions." No doubt a biblical text pried from its context can be twisted to say something very different from what its author actually intended.

The Church's criteria guide us here by defining what constitutes the authentic "context" of a given biblical passage. The first criterion directs us to the literary context of every verse, including not only the words and paragraphs that surround it, but also the entire corpus of the biblical author's writings and, indeed, the span of the entire Bible. The *complete* literary context of any Scripture verse includes every text from Genesis to Revelation—because the Bible is a unified book, not just a library of different books. When the Church canonized the Book of Revelation, for example, she recognized it to be incomprehensible apart from the wider context of the entire Bible.

The second criterion places the Bible firmly within the context of a community that treasures a "living tradition". That community is the People of God down through the ages. Christians lived out their faith for well over a millennium before the printing press was invented. For centuries, few believers owned copies of the Gospels, and few people could read anyway. Yet they absorbed the gospel—through the sermons of their bishops and clergy, through prayer and meditation, through Christian art, through liturgical celebrations, and through oral tradition. These were expressions of the one "living tradition", a culture of living faith that stretches from ancient Israel to the contemporary Church. For the early Christians, the gospel could not be understood apart from that tradition. So it is with us. Reverence for the Church's tradition is what protects us from any sort of chronological or cultural provincialism, such as scholarly fads that arise and carry away a generation of interpreters before being dismissed by the next generation.

The third criterion places scriptural texts within the framework of faith. If we believe that the Scriptures are divinely inspired, we must also believe them to be internally coherent and consistent with all the doctrines that Christians believe. Remember, the Church's dogmas (such as the Real Presence, the papacy, the Immaculate Conception) are not something *added* to Scripture; rather, they are the Church's infallible interpretation *of* Scripture.

Using This Study Guide This volume is designed to lead the reader through Scripture according to the Church's guidelines—faithful to the canon, to the tradition, and to the creeds. The Church's interpretive principles have thus shaped the component parts of this book, and they are designed to make the reader's study as effective and rewarding as possible.

Introductions: We have introduced the biblical book with an essay covering issues such as authorship, date of composition, purpose, and leading themes. This background information will assist readers to approach and understand the text on its own terms.

Annotations: The basic notes at the bottom of every page help the user to read the Scriptures with understanding. They by no means exhaust the meaning of the sacred text but provide background material to help the reader make sense of what he reads. Often these notes make explicit what the sacred writers assumed or held to be implicit. They also provide a great deal of historical, cultural, geographical, and theological information pertinent to the inspired narratives—information that can help the reader bridge the distance between the biblical world and his own.

Cross-References: Between the biblical text at the top of each page and the annotations at the bottom, numerous references are listed to point readers to other scriptural passages related to the one being studied. This follow-up is an essential part of any serious study. It is also an excellent way to discover how the content of Scripture "hangs together" in a providential unity. Along with biblical cross-references, the annotations refer to select paragraphs from the *Catechism of the Catholic Church*. These are not doctrinal "proof texts" but are designed to help the reader interpret the Bible in accordance with the mind of the Church. The *Catechism* references listed either handle the biblical text directly or treat a broader doctrinal theme that sheds significant light on that text.

Topical Essays, Word Studies, Charts: These features bring readers to a deeper understanding of select details. The *topical essays* take up major themes and explain them more thoroughly and theologically than the annotations, often relating them to the doctrines of the Church. Occasionally the annotations are supplemented by *word studies* that put readers in touch with the ancient languages of Scripture. These should help readers to understand better and appreciate the inspired terminology that runs throughout the sacred books. Also included are various *charts* that summarize biblical information "at a glance".

Icon Annotations: Three distinctive icons are interspersed throughout the annotations, each one corresponding to one of the Church's three criteria for biblical interpretation. Bullets indicate the passage or passages to which these icons apply.

Notes marked by the book icon relate to the "content and unity" of Scripture, showing how particular passages of the Old Testament illuminate the mysteries of the New. Much of the information in these notes explains the original context of the citations and indicates how and why this has a direct bearing on Christ or the Church. Through these notes, the reader can develop a sensitivity to the beauty and unity of God's saving plan as it stretches across both Testaments.

Notes marked by the dove icon examine particular passages in light of the Church's "living tradition". Because the Holy Spirit both guides the Magisterium and inspires the spiritual senses of Scripture, these annotations supply information along both of these lines. On the one hand, they refer to the Church's doctrinal teaching as presented by various popes, creeds, and ecumenical councils; on the other, they draw from (and paraphrase) the spiritual interpretations of various Fathers, Doctors, and saints.

Notes marked by the keys icon pertain to the "analogy of faith". Here we spell out how the mysteries of our faith "unlock" and explain one another. This type of comparison between Christian beliefs displays the coherence and unity of defined dogmas, which are the Church's infallible interpretations of Scripture.

Putting It All in Perspective Perhaps the most important context of all we have saved for last:
the interior life of the individual reader. What we get out of the Bible will largely depend on how we approach the Bible. Unless we are living a sustained and disciplined life of prayer, we will never have the reverence, the profound humility, or the grace we need to see the Scriptures for what they really are.

You are approaching the "word of God". But for thousands of years, since before he knit you in your mother's womb, the Word of God has been approaching you.

One Final Note. The volume you hold in your hands is only a small part of a much larger work still in production. Study helps similar to those printed in this booklet are being prepared for *all* the books of the Bible and will appear gradually as they are finished. Our ultimate goal is to publish a single, one-volume Study Bible that will include the entire text of Scripture, along with all the annotations, charts, cross-references, maps, and other features found in the following pages. Individual booklets will be published in the meantime, with the hope that God's people can begin to benefit from this labor before its full completion.

We have included a long list of Study Questions in the back to make this format as useful as possible, not only for individual study, but for group settings and discussions as well. The questions are designed to help readers both "understand" the Bible and "apply" it to their lives. We pray that God will make use of our efforts and yours to help renew the face of the earth! «

INTRODUCTION TO JUDGES

Author and Date Like all the Historical Books of the Old Testament, the Book of Judges was written anonymously. Jewish tradition ascribed its authorship to the prophet Samuel (Babylonian Talmud, *Baba Bathra* 14b). This is not impossible, but it remains unlikely that scholars will ever be able to verify the tradition conclusively. Remarks can be made about the writer's theological outlook and interests, and inferences have been drawn regarding his genealogy (probably a tribesman of Judah), but at present we cannot confidently attach to the author the name of a known historical figure.

The date of the book is likewise uncertain, although a few clues regarding the time of its composition can be discovered within its pages. The most promising indicators point to an origin early in the monarchical period, perhaps around 1005 B.C. Evidence suggestive of this historical setting includes the following: **(1)** Several times the writer characterizes the era of the judges as a tumultuous time when "there was no king in Israel" (17:6; 18:1; 19:1; 21:25). Scholars generally take this to mean that the author lived after the founding of the Israelite monarchy in the mid-eleventh century B.C., when the practical benefits of kingship were both felt and appreciated on a national scale. **(2)** The author states that "the Jebusites have dwelt with the people of Benjamin in Jerusalem to this day" (1:21). Such a comment would be unlikely to stand without remark after David wrested Jerusalem from Jebusite control and made it Israel's capital city around 1004 B.C. **(3)** Most telling of all, the book has political undertones that seem to indicate that the tense rivalry between King Saul (of the tribe of Benjamin) and King David (of the tribe of Judah) was a live issue at the time of writing. Consider, for instance, how Judges casts a shadow over the ancestry of Saul by underlining the failure of the Benjaminites to capture Jerusalem (1:21) and by exposing the depravity of the Benjaminites to the point of singling out Saul's hometown of Gibeah for rebuke (19:10–26). This is in marked contrast to the book's positive portrayal of David's ancestors. His own tribe of Judah was the first to make successful conquests in its assigned territory (1:1–20), the first to conquer Jerusalem (1:21), the first to produce a judge to deliver Israel (3:7–11), and the first to take action against the Benjaminite perpetrators of evil (20:18). And unlike Saul's hometown of Gibeah, which proved to be inhospitable in the extreme (19:10–26), David's hometown of Bethlehem shows every kindness to its visitors (19:1–9). In these and other ways, the Book of Judges shows partisan preference for the house of David over the house of Saul, and the most relevant historical context for this interest is near the end of the eleventh century B.C.

Modern critical scholarship has generated multiple theories regarding the origin of Judges. Many acknowledge that the book incorporates ancient stories and poems, a few of which are traceable to the second millennium B.C. (e.g., the Song of Deborah in 5:2–31), but there is a strong tendency to date the final form of the book to the Babylonian Exile in the sixth century B.C. The main reason is that Judges is said to form a literary and theological unity with the collection of biblical texts from Joshua to 2 Kings (minus Ruth). These works, conventionally called the Deuteronomistic History, form a retrospective account of Israel's national story from the people's entrance into the land (Conquest of Canaan) to their expulsion from the land (Babylonian Exile). Not only are these books held together around a connected timeline, which explains why they are placed side by side in the OT canon, but each is stamped with the distinctive theology and language of the Book of Deuteronomy to one degree or another. And since this historical narrative concludes in 2 Kings with Judah's deportation to Babylon in 586 B.C., this date represents the approximate time at which the collection was last edited and given its canonical form.

Together these observations suggest that the Book of Judges passed through more than one stage of composition. Given the mixture of early and late features in the book, it is reasonable to postulate a *first* edition of the Book of Judges in the early monarchical period, when an unnamed compiler gathered into a single work stories and poems that had long circulated as oral or written tradition among the Israelite tribes, and then a *final* edition of the book in the exilic period, when an unnamed editor put the finishing touches on the text, drawing attention to the connection between Israel's national experiences and the teaching of Deuteronomy. In the end, much remains to be clarified, and so all hypotheses regarding the formation of the Book of Judges are necessarily provisional.

Title The Hebrew title of the book is *shophetim*, "Judges". This term, which appears first in 2:16, refers to intermittent leaders raised up by God during the extended period of Israel's settlement of Canaan. A few of the biblical judges served as arbitrators and dispensers of legal justice, as the

English term suggests, but many were warriors and tribal deliverers. The Hebrew heading is reproduced in the Greek Septuagint as *Kritai*, "Judges", whereas the Latin Vulgate supplies the fuller title *Liber Iudicum*, "Book of Judges".

Place in the Canon Judges follows Joshua in the order of Old Testament books because it continues the biblical story after the death of Joshua (1:1). In the Hebrew Bible, it is the second of the "Former Prophets", the name given to the books of Joshua, Judges, Samuel, and Kings. These volumes relate the history of God's people from the standpoint of the prophets, whose overriding concern is Israel's covenant with the Lord and how the state of this relationship determines the fate of the nation for good or ill. Christian tradition regards Judges as one of the "Historical Books" of Scripture without disputing its theological or prophetic character.

Structure Judges follows a basic threefold outline. **(1)** The book opens with a *prologue*: its first half, 1:1—2:5, reports on the status of the Conquest after the passing of Joshua, and its second half, 2:6—3:6, offers a theological diagnosis in which Israel's apostasy and idolatry are exposed as the underlying causes of its troubles during this period. **(2)** The *main body* of the book extends from 3:7—16:31. This section consists of stories and short notices that revolve around twelve judges whom the Lord raises up to rescue Israel from the yoke of foreign oppression. Six of these figures are major judges whose stories are told in some detail (Othniel, Ehud, Deborah, Gideon, Jephthah, Samson), while six others are minor judges whose heroism is mentioned only briefly (Shamgar, Tola, Jair, Ibzan, Elon, Abdon). **(3)** The book closes with an *epilogue*: its first half, 17:1—18:31, presents a glaring example of the spiritual disorder that reigned during the time of the judges, and its second half, 19:1—21:25, gives a disturbing account of the moral depravity that thrived alongside it.

Themes and Characteristics The Book of Judges covers the historical period between the death of Joshua and the birth of Samuel. These were dark and turbulent times as Israel rode the pendulum back and forth between prosperity and adversity, between the blessings and curses of the covenant. Thanks to Joshua and his generation, the twelve tribes had firmly established themselves in parts of the Promised Land. But because of a chronic failure to serve Yahweh faithfully and exclusively, succeeding generations were unsuccessful in gaining full possession of their homeland and were frequently harassed by their enemies. In many ways, the stories of victory and hope that rang out in the Book of Joshua are now muffled by the stories of defeat and discouragement that weigh down the Book of Judges.

Perhaps the most notable feature in Judges is the cycle of rebellion and restoration that emerges from the main body of the book. Time and again we see Israel *sinning* against the Lord, being *subjugated* by foreign powers, and crying out for *salvation*. This sequence repeats itself seven times in the book and is marked off by recurring formulas that stand at the beginning and end of the cycles. Each rotation begins with the Israelites doing "evil in the sight of the Lord" (2:11; 3:7, 12; 4:1; 6:1; 10:6; 13:1), and each rotation ends either with the number of years "the land had rest" (3:11, 30; 5:31; 8:28) or with the number of years the hero in question "judged Israel" (12:7; 15:20; 16:31).

Evident in these cycles of disobedience, distress, and deliverance is the weakness of Israel as well as the mercy of Yahweh. Despite incurring divine discipline in the form of invasion, oppression, and war, the Israelites are quick to abandon the Lord for other gods and to shirk the obligations of the covenant. Repentance is always shallow and short-lived, and a return to godless ways soon follows the period of respite provided by the judges. Thankfully, the persistent failures of Israel are outmatched by the persistent faithfulness of Yahweh. The God of Israel never forsakes his struggling people but is ever gracious and ready to save. The judges, summoned to rescue the covenant people from suffering, stand as living proof of the Lord's extraordinary patience and compassion. The covenant bond uniting God and Israel, though repeatedly tested, is repeatedly affirmed.

Surprisingly, the judges themselves were deeply flawed individuals who did little to stem the tide of Israel's infidelity. On the one hand, they were tasked with delivering Israel from tribal threats as agents of Yahweh, the divine Judge (11:27). On the other hand, theirs was not an overtly spiritual ministry. No doubt the judges exercised genuine faith in certain situations, as noted in Heb 11:32–34, and yet they were generally tainted by the same forms of corruption that plagued the nation as a whole. It seems that highlighting the failings of Israel's tribal heroes was meant to throw the goodness of Israel's God into greater relief. It shows that the Lord's desire to bless his people is not limited by the imperfections of the men and women he raises up to participate in his work.

Besides displaying defects of character, most of the judges appear to have been unlikely candidates for leadership. They were the kinds of persons whom ancient societies least expected to do great things. Shamgar, for instance, made himself a legendary warrior by wielding a farmer's tool rather than armaments forged for battle. Deborah was a woman wielding authority in a predominately patriarchal world. Gideon was a cowardly figure from one of the weakest clans of his tribe. Jephthah was born to a prostitute. Samson was mighty in stature but pathetically weak in guarding his purity and maintaining his religious vows. And virtually no one from the ministerial tribe of Levi or the royal tribe of Judah stepped forward to lead Israel in faithful observance of the covenant. Instead, everyone "did what was right in his own eyes" (21:25). Such was the confusion of the times.

From a canonical perspective, the Book of Judges may be said to set the stage for the founding of the Davidic monarchy. Attention is repeatedly drawn to the fact that Israel had "no king" at this stage in biblical history (17:6; 18:1; 19:1; 21:25). Implicit in this refrain is the claim that anarchy is a problem in need of a practical solution. While theocracy remains an ideal, with the Lord as King administering his rule by means of the covenant, Israel has need of something that is tailored to its weaknesses. The Book of Judges is propelling the story to the critical point where Yahweh will concede to establish a monarchy (in 1 Samuel) and a hereditary covenant of kingship with David (in 2 Samuel). Royal government, though not without its drawbacks, is anticipated as a stabilizing institution that can help to bring lawlessness under control and a civilizing institution that can help to draw Israel to higher moral and spiritual ground. For the relationship between the accounts of Judges and Joshua, see Introduction to Joshua: *Themes*.

Christian Perspective The Book of Judges is never quoted directly in the New Testament, but reference is made to it in other ways. For instance, several of its heroes are named and admired for their faith in Heb 11:32. Likewise, echoes of its ancient stories can be heard in the background of select Gospel stories. For example, details surrounding the birth of Samson likewise surround the birth of John the Baptist, suggesting the former was viewed as prefiguring the latter (compare 13:2–5 and 16:17 with Lk 1:5–15). Likewise, the words of Deborah that extol the heroine Jael are nearly the same words that Elizabeth uses to praise Mary, the mother of Jesus (compare 5:24 with Lk 1:42). Allegorically, Christian faith sees the judges as types of the messianic Judge to come, Jesus Christ. For all these figures, acting as saviors and deliverers, are raised up by the mercy of God to fight off the enemies of God and to restore peace to the People of God. Morally, the account of Israel struggling to break the cycle of sin and repentance may be said to dramatize the recurring struggles of the Christian spiritual life, where lessons of faith and obedience are often learned by the humbling experience of failure and forgiveness.

OUTLINE OF JUDGES

1. Prologue (1:1—3:6)
    A. Conquest and Coexistence in Canaan (1:1—2:5)
    B. Israel's Apostasy and Idolatry (2:6—3:6)

2. The Main Body (3:7—16:31)
    A. The Judges Othniel, Ehud, and Shamgar (3:7–31)
    B. The Judge Deborah and the Song of Deborah (4:1—5:31)
    C. The Judge Gideon and the Anti-Judge Abimelech (6:1—9:57)
    D. The Judges Tola and Jair (10:1–18)
    E. The Judges Jephthah, Ibzan, Elon, Abdon (11:1—12:15)
    F. The Judge Samson (13:1—16:31)

3. Epilogue (17:1—21:25)
    A. Micah and the Levite (17:1–13)
    B. The Danite Migration (18:1–31)
    C. Wickedness of the Benjaminites (19:1–30)
    D. War on the Benjaminites (20:1–48)
    E. Preservation of the Benjaminites (21:1–25)

THE BOOK OF

JUDGES

Israel's Failure to Complete the Conquest

1 *After the death of Joshua the sons of Israel inquired of the Lord, "Who shall go up first for us against the Canaanites, to fight against them?" ²The Lord said, "Judah shall go up; behold, I have given the land into his hand." ³And Judah said to Simeon his brother, "Come up with me into the territory allotted to me, that we may fight against the Canaanites; and I likewise will go with you into the territory allotted to you." So Simeon went with him. ⁴Then Judah went up and the Lord gave the Canaanites and the Per'izzites into their hand; and they defeated ten thousand of them at Be'zek. ⁵They came upon Ado'ni-be'zek at Be'zek, and fought against him, and defeated the Canaanites and the Per'izzites. ⁶Ado'ni-be'zek fled; but they pursued him, and caught him, and cut off his thumbs and his great toes. ⁷And Ado'ni-be'zek said, "Seventy kings with their thumbs and their great toes cut off used to pick up scraps under my table; as I have done, so God has repaid me." And they brought him to Jerusalem, and he died there.

8 And the men of Judah fought against Jerusalem, and took it, and struck it with the edge of the sword, and set the city on fire. ⁹And afterward the men of Judah went down to fight against the Canaanites who dwelt in the hill country, in the Neg'eb, and in the lowland. ¹⁰And Judah went against the Canaanites who dwelt in He'bron (now the name of Hebron was formerly Kir'iath-ar'ba); and they defeated Sheshai and Ahi'man and Talmai.

11 From there they went against the inhabitants of De'bir. The name of Debir was formerly Kir'iath-se'pher. ¹²And Caleb said, "He who attacks Kir'iath-se'pher and takes it, I will give him Ach'sah my daughter as wife." ¹³And Oth'ni-el the son of Ke'naz, Caleb's younger brother, took it; and he gave him Ach'sah his daughter as wife. ¹⁴When she came to him, she urged him to ask her father for a field; and she alighted from her donkey, and Caleb said to her, "What do you wish?" ¹⁵She said to him, "Give me a present; since you have set me in the land of the Neg'eb, give me also springs of water." And Caleb gave her the upper springs and the lower springs.

16 And the descendants of the Ken'ite, Moses' father-in-law, went up with the people of Judah from the city of palms into the wilderness of

---

1:10: Josh 15:13–19.   **1:10-15**: Josh 15:14–19.

1:1–2:5 Judges opens with a status report on the progress of the Conquest following the death of Joshua. Limited success is achieved by the tribes of Judah and Simeon in subduing parts of southern Canaan and by the house of Joseph in central Canaan, but Benjamin and the northern tribes of Israel generally fail to secure their allotted territories. At the level of literary composition, there is a broad correspondence between the sequence of tribes listed in Judges 1 (Judah, Simeon, Benjamin, Manasseh, Ephraim, Zebulun, Asher, Naphtali, Dan) and the tribes that produce major judges in Judges 3–16: Judah (Othniel), Benjamin (Ehud), Ephraim (Deborah), Manasseh (Gideon, Jephthah), and Dan (Samson).

1:1 the death of Joshua: Recorded in Josh 24:29–30. The event is a turning point signaling that Israel is now leaderless as a nation. **inquired of the Lord:** Presumably by means of the sacred lots, Urim and Thummim, kept in a vestment worn by the high priest (Ex 28:30; Num 27:18–21). **go up:** Israel appears to be gathered near Jericho according to 1:16, so any expedition into other parts of Canaan would require an uphill march out of the Jordan Valley.

1:3 Judah: Allotted tribal territory in southern Canaan (Josh 15:1–12). **Simeon:** Allotted several cities within the borders of Judah's territory (Josh 19:1–9).

1:4 Bezek: Exact location uncertain but likely in the highlands northwest of Jerusalem.

1:7 Seventy kings: Reflects accurately the political situation of pre-Israelite Canaan, which was made up of numerous city-states governed by local monarchs. See note on Josh 2:2.

1:8 Jerusalem: An ancient Jebusite stronghold on the tribal border between Judah and Benjamin (Josh 18:28). Neither tribe was able to claim it decisively in the early settlement period (1:21; Josh 15:63). Here Judah overthrows the city and occupies it for a time, but evidently the Jebusites recapture the site afterward. David will be the first to make Jerusalem a permanent Israelite city (2 Sam 5:6–10).

1:9 Negeb: The arid region stretching across the deep south of Canaan.

1:10 Hebron: About 20 miles south of Jerusalem. **Sheshai ... Ahiman ... Talmai:** Three clans named after the three warrior sons of Anak (Num 13:28). For background, see note on Josh 11:21.

1:11–15 Retells the story of Josh 15:13–19.

1:11 Debir: Over seven miles southwest of Hebron in southern Canaan.

1:16 the Kenite: Father of a clan of Midianites whose descendants settled alongside Judah in southeast Canaan. The relationship between Israel and the Kenites goes back to Moses' intermarriage with the Midianites in Ex 2:15-21 as well as the encounter in Num 10:29-32, where Moses promised to share God's blessings with certain Midianites in exchange for knowledgeable guidance through the wilderness. Scholars infer from the name that the Kenites were probably metalsmiths. **Moses' father-in-law:** Known both as Jethro (Ex 3:1; 18:1) and as Reuel (Ex 2:18; Num 10:29). See note on 4:11. **city of palms:** Jericho, six miles north of the Dead Sea in the western Jordan Valley (Deut 34:3).

This book, which has been edited at least twice, fills in the period from the settlement to the monarchy. This was a period of crisis that gave rise to "saviors" raised up by God to meet these critical situations. The deeds of six of these are recounted at some length: Othniel, Ehud, Deborah (and Barak), Gideon, Jephthah, Samson; there are also six "minor" judges who are given only a short notice: Shamgar, Tola, Jair, Ibzan, Elon, Abdon. The book ends with two appendixes (chapters 17–21).

*1:1: This first chapter describes the difficulties and defeats of the conquest.

Judah, which lies in the Negeb near Ar'ad; and they went and settled with the people. ¹⁷And Judah went with Simeon his brother, and they defeated the Canaanites who inhabited Ze'phath, and utterly destroyed it. So the name of the city was called Hormah. ¹⁸Judah also took Gaza with its territory, and Ash'kelon with its territory, and Ek'ron with its territory. ¹⁹And the LORD was with Judah, and he took possession of the hill country, but he could not drive out the inhabitants of the plain, because they had chariots of iron. ²⁰And He'bron was given to Caleb, as Moses had said; and he drove out from it the three sons of A'nak. ²¹But the people of Benjamin did not drive out the Jeb'usites who dwelt in Jerusalem; so the Jebusites have dwelt with the people of Benjamin in Jerusalem to this day.

22 The house of Joseph also went up against Bethel; and the LORD was with them. ²³And the house of Joseph sent to spy out Bethel. (Now the name of the city was formerly Luz.) ²⁴And the spies saw a man coming out of the city, and they said to him, "Please, show us the way into the city, and we will deal kindly with you." ²⁵And he showed them the way into the city; and they struck the city with the edge of the sword, but they let the man and all his family go. ²⁶And the man went to the land of the Hittites and built a city, and called its name Luz; that is its name to this day.

27 Manas'seh did not drive out the inhabitants of Beth-she'an and its villages, or Ta'anach and its villages, or the inhabitants of Dor and its villages, or the inhabitants of Ib'leam and its villages, or the inhabitants of Megid'do and its villages, but the Canaanites persisted in dwelling in that land. ²⁸When Israel grew strong, they put the Canaanites to forced labor, but did not utterly drive them out.

29 And E'phraim did not drive out the Canaanites who dwelt in Gezer; but the Canaanites dwelt in Gezer among them.

30 Zeb'ulun did not drive out the inhabitants of Kitron, or the inhabitants of Nahal'ol; but the Canaanites dwelt among them, and became subject to forced labor.

31 Asher did not drive out the inhabitants of Ac'co, or the inhabitants of Si'don, or of Ahlab, or of Ach'zib, or of Helbah, or of A'phik, or of Re'hob; ³²but the Ash'erites dwelt among the Canaanites, the inhabitants of the land; for they did not drive them out.

33 Naph'tali did not drive out the inhabitants of Beth-she'mesh, or the inhabitants of Beth-a'nath, but dwelt among the Canaanites, the inhabitants of the land; nevertheless the inhabitants of Beth-shemesh and of Beth-anath became subject to forced labor for them.

34 The Am'orites pressed the Da'nites back into the hill country, for they did not allow them to come down to the plain; ³⁵the Am'orites persisted in dwelling in Har-he'res, in Ai'jalon, and in Sha-al'bim, but the hand of the house of Joseph rested heavily upon them, and they became subject to forced labor. ³⁶And the border of the Am'orites ran from the ascent of Akrab'bim, from Se'la and upward.

1:20: Josh 15:14. **1:21:** Josh 15:63. **1:27, 28:** Josh 17:11–13. **1:29:** Josh 16:10.

1:17 Hormah: Means "destruction". It is related to a military term used throughout the Conquest narratives, on which see Word Study: *Devoted* at Josh 6:17.

1:18 Gaza ... Ashkelon ... Ekron: Cities in southwest Canaan later controlled by Philistines.

1:19 the LORD was with Judah: Divine favor explains the tribe's success in conquering and settling most of its assigned territory. **chariots of iron:** Wooden chariots with iron fittings and coverings. Judah seems to think itself outmatched by the military superiority of the coastland Canaanites, despite the promise in Josh 17:18.

1:20 three sons of Anak: Their names appear in 1:10.

1:21 people of Benjamin: Unable to wrest control of Jerusalem from its native inhabitants and so unable to claim any notable accomplishment at this time. The same is true of the people of Judah (Josh 15:63) until they eventually mount a successful attack on the city (1:8). **Jebusites:** One of several Gentile peoples who lived in Canaan before Israel's arrival (Gen 15:18–21). See note on 1:8.

1:22–36 Israel's central and northern tribes do more to compromise with their enemies than conquer them. Joseph, mentioned first, is the most successful (1:22–26), while Dan, mentioned last, is the least successful (1:34–36). The dire consequences of an incomplete Conquest will be felt by Israel throughout the rest of the book.

1:22 Joseph: Refers to the tribes of Ephraim and Manasseh, whose territories cover central Canaan.

1:23–26 The takeover of Bethel recalls the conquest of Jericho. • In both stories, spies from Israel make contact with an individual from the city (Josh 2:1), establish a covenant of nonaggression with the informant in exchange for military intelligence (Josh 2:12–14), and spare the family of the defector when the city is sacked (Josh 6:22–23). A critical difference is that Rahab professes faith in Yahweh and joins the assembly of Israel (Josh 2:11; 6:25), whereas the man from Bethel retains his Canaanite identity and refounds the city elsewhere (1:26).

1:23 Bethel: Roughly ten miles north of Jerusalem. Archaeology has long located Bethel at modern Beitin, although a somewhat stronger case has been made for the site of Bireh. Bethel, which means "house of God", had been consecrated to the worship of Yahweh since patriarchal times (Gen 12:8; 28:18–22; 35:6–7).

1:24 deal kindly: A promise to show loyalty to partners in a covenant.

1:26 land of the Hittites: Possibly a reference to Syria (rather than Asia Minor).

1:27 did not drive out: Implies that Israel stops short of full obedience to the Lord, who commanded the elimination of Canaan's pagan population (Deut 7:1–2; 20:16–18). **Beth-shean ... Megiddo:** Settlements in lower Galilee.

1:28 forced labor: Canaanites not destroyed or dislodged from the land are subjugated as slaves (1:30, 33, 35). Positively, this is evidence of Israel's superior strength; negatively, Israel's willingness to settle for coexistence with the native peoples will put the nation at great spiritual risk. For the significance of Canaanite enslavement, see note on Josh 16:10.

1:36 the Amorites: Here a reference to Canaanite peoples still dwelling near Edom, south of the Dead Sea (cf. Deut 1:44).

Israel's Disobedience

2 Now the angel of the Lord went up from Gilgal to Bochim. And he said, "I brought you up from Egypt, and brought you into the land which I swore to give to your fathers. I said, 'I will never break my covenant with you, ²and you shall make no covenant with the inhabitants of this land; you shall break down their altars.' But you have not obeyed my command. What is this you have done? ³So now I say, I will not drive them out before you; but they shall become adversaries[a] to you, and their gods shall be a snare to you." ⁴When the angel of the Lord spoke these words to all the sons of Israel, the people lifted up their voices and wept. ⁵And they called the name of that place Bochim;[b] and they sacrificed there to the Lord.

Death of Joshua

6 When Joshua dismissed the people, the sons of Israel went each to his inheritance to take possession of the land. ⁷And the people served the Lord all the days of Joshua, and all the days of the elders who outlived Joshua, who had seen all the great work which the Lord had done for Israel. ⁸And Joshua the son of Nun, the servant of the Lord, died at the age of one hundred and ten years. ⁹And they buried him within the bounds of his inheritance in Tim′nath-he′res, in the hill country of E′phraim, north of the mountain of Ga′ash. ¹⁰And all that generation also were gathered to their fathers; and there arose another generation after them, who did not know the Lord or the work which he had done for Israel.

Israel's Unfaithfulness

11 And the sons of Israel did what was evil in the sight of the Lord and served the Ba′als; ¹²and they forsook the Lord, the God of their fathers, who had brought them out of the land of Egypt; they went after other gods, from among the gods of the peoples who were round about them, and bowed down to them; and they provoked the Lord to anger. ¹³They forsook the Lord, and served the Ba′als and the Ash′taroth. ¹⁴So the anger of the Lord was kindled against Israel, and he gave them over to plunderers, who plundered them; and he sold them into the power of their enemies round about, so that they could no longer withstand their enemies. ¹⁵Whenever they marched out, the hand of the Lord was against them for evil, as the Lord had warned, and as the Lord had sworn to them; and they were in great distress.

16 Then the Lord raised up judges, who saved them out of the power of those who plundered them. ¹⁷And yet they did not listen to their judges; for they played the harlot after other gods and bowed down to them; they soon turned aside from the way in which their fathers had walked, who had obeyed the commandments of the Lord, and they did not do so. ¹⁸Whenever the Lord raised up judges for them, the Lord was with the judge, and he saved them from the hand of their enemies all the days of the judge; for the Lord was moved to pity by their groaning because of those who afflicted and oppressed them. ¹⁹But whenever the judge died, they turned back and behaved worse than their fathers, going after other gods, serving them and bowing down

---

2:6–9: Josh 24:28–31.

2:1 angel of the Lord: A divine messenger who speaks and acts in the name of Yahweh. This figure may be an angel who appears in human form, although the underlying Hebrew expression can also be used of a prophet (as in Hag 1:3). See word study: *Angel of the Lord* at Gen 16:7. **Gilgal:** In the western Jordan Valley near Jericho. Gilgal was the site of Israel's base camp when the Conquest began (Josh 4:19). **Bochim:** Means "weepers" and likely refers to the town of Bethel, recently made an Israelite settlement (1:22–26). Israel is again seen weeping at Bethel near the end of the book (20:26). • *Allegorically*, the valley of weeping is a reference to this world, since we are not on the mountain, which is the kingdom of heaven, but down in the darkness of this world. Along with Adam we have been cast forth from paradise into a valley of tears, where there is repentance (St. Jerome, *Homilies* 63).

2:2 make no covenant: Commanded in Ex 23:32. **break down their altars:** Commanded in Ex 34:14.

2:4 the people ... wept: A sign of remorse but not of authentic repentance, as the rest of the book makes clear (CCC 1451).

2:6–10 A flashback to Josh 24:28–31 and the passing of the Conquest generation.

2:11—3:6 A theological preface to the stories in Judges 3–16. It outlines briefly the cycle of sin, suffering, and salvation that will dominate the accounts of the judges and their exploits. The lesson is twofold: (1) violation of the covenant, especially idolatry, is the root cause of Israel's frustration during this period (CCC 2112–14), and (2) the Lord of the covenant is prepared to show relentless mercy each time his people cry out for relief (CCC 211, 270). • These verses, more than any other in the book, are shaped by the theological vision and vocabulary of Deuteronomy (see especially Deut 4:25; 6:14; 8:6, 19; 9:3; 17:2).

2:11 Baals: Baal is the storm and fertility god of Canaanite religion. In Semitic mythology, he rides the clouds as a chariot, wields lightning as a weapon, and makes his voice heard in thunder. Baal was extremely important to the agricultural life of Canaan, as he was believed to bring the rains after every dry season. Here the name is plural because worship of Baal takes place at multiple sites throughout Canaan.

2:13 Ashtaroth: The plural of Ashtoreth, the name of the mother goddess of love, war, and fertility. Her name is rendered "Astarte" in Greek and "Ishtar" in Akkadian. Figurines of her image have turned up at numerous archaeological sites in Palestine.

2:16 judges: Twelve appear in the book, six major judges (Othniel, Ehud, Deborah, Gideon, Jephthah, Samson) and six minor judges (Shamgar, Tola, Jair, Ibzan, Elon, Abdon). See chart: *Victories of the Judges* in chap. 3.

2:17 played the harlot: Idolatry is a form of spiritual prostitution (Ex 34:15).

2:18 groaning: Recalls the groaning of Israel on the eve of the Exodus (Ex 2:23–24; 6:5).

---

[a] Vg Old Latin Compare Gk: Heb *sides*.
[b] That is *Weepers*.

to them; they did not drop any of their practices or their stubborn ways.* ²⁰So the anger of the LORD was kindled against Israel; and he said, "Because this people have transgressed my covenant which I commanded their fathers, and have not obeyed my voice, ²¹from now on I will not drive out before them any of the nations that Joshua left when he died, ²²that by them I may test Israel, whether they will take care to walk in the way of the LORD as their fathers did, or not." ²³So the LORD left those nations, not driving them out at once, and he did not give them into the power of Joshua.

Nations Remaining in the Land

3 Now these are the nations which the LORD left, to test Israel by them, that is, all in Israel who had no experience of any war in Canaan; ²it was only that the generations of the sons of Israel might know war, that he might teach war to such at least as had not known it before. ³These are the nations: the five lords of the Philis′tines, and all the Canaanites, and the Sido′nians, and the Hi′vites who dwelt on Mount Lebanon, from Mount Ba′al-her′mon as far as the entrance of Ha′math. ⁴They were for the testing of Israel, to know whether Israel would obey the commandments of the LORD, which he commanded their fathers by Moses. ⁵So the sons of Israel dwelt among the Canaanites, the Hittites, the Am′orites, the Per′izzites, the Hi′vites, and the Jeb′usites; ⁶and they took their daughters to themselves for wives, and their own daughters they gave to their sons; and they served their gods.

Othni-el

7 And the sons of Israel did what was evil in the sight of the LORD, forgetting the LORD their God, and serving the Ba′als and the Ashe′roth. ⁸Therefore the anger of the LORD was kindled against Israel, and he sold them into the hand of Cu′shan-rishatha′im king of Mesopota′mia; and the sons of Israel served Cushan-rishathaim eight years. ⁹But when the sons of Israel cried to the LORD, the LORD raised up a deliverer for the sons of Israel, who delivered them, Oth′ni-el the son of Ke′naz, Caleb's younger brother. ¹⁰The Spirit of the LORD came upon him, and he judged Israel; he went out to war, and the LORD gave Cu′shan-rishatha′im king of Mesopota′mia into his hand; and his hand prevailed over Cushan-rishathaim. ¹¹So the land had rest forty years. Then Oth′ni-el the son of Ke′naz died.

2:22 test Israel: Scripture offers at least five reasons why the settlement of Canaan is a long and drawn-out process. Although the Lord could have wiped out the Canaanites at a stroke, he leaves survivors in the land in order **(1)** to test the loyalty of Israel under the pressure to live and worship like the pagans (2:21–22), **(2)** to teach future generations of Israel the lessons of holy war (3:1–2), **(3)** to discipline Israel for sins against the covenant (3:7–8, 12–14; etc.), **(4)** to ensure that Canaan, overwhelmed by war, will not be overrun by beasts (Deut 7:22), and **(5)** to give the doomed population of Canaan time to repent of their wickedness (Wis 12:3–11).

3:2 teach war: The goal is not only to provide military training but to strengthen the faith of later generations as they witness Yahweh's power in giving Israel victories on the battlefield.

3:3 the nations: Occupied western Canaan as well as its northernmost territory. Israel was settled on both sides of the Jordan River and in firm possession of the central hill country. **Philistines:** Part of a mixed group of "Sea Peoples" who migrated to the Near East in the late second millennium B.C. According to the Bible, the Philistines came from the Aegean island of Crete (called "Caphtor", Deut 2:23; Jer 47:4; Amos 9:7), although Genesis indicates they had more ancient ties with the Hamitic peoples of northeast Africa (Gen 10:6–14). Following a series of military clashes with Egypt in the early 1100s B.C., they settled in southwest Canaan and established a coalition of five prominent cities (Ekron, Ashdod, Ashkelon, Gaza, and Gath). The Philistines are determined enemies of Israel in the time of the judges and the days of the early monarchy (3:31; 13:1; 14:4; 1 Sam 4:1; 13:3; etc.). **Canaanites:** Controlled much of the western coastal plain "by the sea" (Josh 5:1). **Sidonians:** Occupied the Phoenician coast northwest of Israel. **Baal-Hermon:** Mount Hermon, northeast of the Sea of Galilee. Baal is the name of a Canaanite god. See note

on 2:11. **Hamath:** At the northeastern border of the Promised Land (Num 34:8).

3:5 Canaanites ... Jebusites: For the nations that occupied Canaan before Israel, see note on Ex 3:8.

3:6 took their daughters: In defiance of God's command to have no involvement, marital or political, with the Canaanites (Deut 7:1–3). The issue at stake was religious purity rather than racial or genealogical purity, for the Lord knew that intermarriage with pagans would drag Israel into idolatry (Deut 7:4) (CCC 1634).

3:7 Baals: Various representations of a single Canaanite deity. See note on 2:11. **Asheroth:** The plural of Asherah, the name of a Canaanite fertility goddess who was revered under the form of a tree or wooden pole erected beside pagan altars (6:25; Deut 16:21).

3:8 Cushan-rishathaim: Means "Cushan the Doubly Wicked". **served:** Repetition of the same verb (Heb., *'abad*) in 3:7 and 3:8 shows that Yahweh punishes service to foreign deities with service to foreign oppressors. See word study: *Serve* at Ex 4:23.

3:9 Othniel: Nephew of the illustrious Caleb, the spy from Judah (Num 34:19) whose faith earned him entrance into the Promised Land (Num 14:30). Earlier, Othniel sacked the city of Debir (1:11–13), and now he leads the effort to drive invaders from Mesopotamia out of Israel (3:10). Othniel is the most exemplary of the judges in the book (along with Deborah), which is to say he has no obvious flaws or shortcomings. In fact, although wayward Israelites begin to intermarry with the Canaanites (3:6), Othniel is wedded to a woman of Judah (1:13).

3:10 Spirit of the LORD: Brings the power of heaven upon the judges and equips them to bring salvation to Israel. The Spirit chooses these figures to participate in divine redemption by preparing their hearts (13:25), by prompting them to take action against the enemy (6:34; 11:29), and, in some cases, by empowering them to perform superhuman feats of bravery and strength (14:6, 19; 15:14) (CCC 702, 2003). • The work of the Spirit in the lives of the judges anticipates the greater work of the Spirit in the coming Messiah. This is foreseen by the prophet Isaiah (Is 61:1–2) and fulfilled in Jesus Christ (Lk 4:16–21).

---

*2:11–19: This passage gives the theological scheme of the book according to which the episodic history is presented. It comes from an editor inspired by the ideas of Deuteronomy and resembles closely the scheme according to which the kings, beginning with Solomon, are assessed and judged.

Ehud

12 And the sons of Israel again did what was evil in the sight of the LORD; and the LORD strengthened Eg′lon the king of Moab against Israel, because they had done what was evil in the sight of the LORD. ¹³He gathered to himself the Am′monites and the Amal′ekites, and went and defeated Israel; and they took possession of the city of palms. ¹⁴And the sons of Israel served Eg′lon the king of Moab eighteen years.

15 But when the sons of Israel cried to the LORD, the LORD raised up for them a deliverer, E′hud, the son of Gera, the Benjaminite, a left-handed man. The sons of Israel sent tribute by him to Eg′lon the king of Moab. ¹⁶And E′hud made for himself a sword with two edges, a cubit in length; and he girded it on his right thigh under his clothes. ¹⁷And he presented the tribute to Eg′lon king of Moab. Now Eglon was a very fat man. ¹⁸And when E′hud had finished presenting the tribute, he sent away the people that carried the tribute. ¹⁹But he himself turned back at the sculptured stones near Gilgal, and said, "I have a secret message for you, O king." And he commanded, "Silence." And all his attendants went out from his presence. ²⁰And E′hud came to him, as he was sitting alone in his cool roof chamber. And Ehud said, "I have a message from God for you." And he arose from his seat. ²¹And

E′hud reached with his left hand, took the sword from his right thigh, and thrust it into his belly; ²²and the hilt also went in after the blade, and the fat closed over the blade, for he did not draw the sword out of his belly; and the dirt came out. ²³Then E′hud went out into the vestibule, c and closed the doors of the roof chamber upon him, and locked them.

24 When he had gone, the servants came; and when they saw that the doors of the roof chamber were locked, they thought, "He is only relieving himself in the closet of the cool chamber." ²⁵And they waited till they were utterly at a loss; but when he still did not open the doors of the roof chamber, they took the key and opened them; and there lay their lord dead on the floor.

26 E′hud escaped while they delayed, and passed beyond the sculptured stones, and escaped to Se-i′rah. ²⁷When he arrived, he sounded the trumpet in the hill country of E′phraim; and the sons of Israel went down with him from the hill country, having him at their head. ²⁸And he said to them, "Follow after me; for the LORD has given your enemies the Moabites into your hand." So they went down after him, and seized the fords of the Jordan against the Moabites, and allowed no man to pass over. ²⁹And they killed at that time about ten thousand of the Moabites, all strong, able-bodied men; not a man escaped. ³⁰So Moab was subdued that day under

---

3:12 again did: Or, possibly, "continued to do". **Eglon:** Means "bull calf". Israelite readers would imagine the obese king as fattened and ready for slaughter. The entire story pokes fun at Eglon, targeting not only his bloated body but also his weak and gullible mind. **Moab:** Southeast of the Dead Sea. See note on Deut 2:9.

3:13 Ammonites: Driven from farmable lands east of the Jordan by the incoming Israelites under Moses (Num 21:21–24). **Amalekites:** Nomads and enemies of Israel who roam the Sinai Peninsula (Ex 17:8–16). **city of palms:** Jericho (Deut 34:3).

3:15 Ehud: Benjaminite warrior and undercover assassin. Disguised as a diplomat bringing tribute, he frees Israel from 18 years of vassalage to the Moabites by stabbing their king in secret (3:15–23) and leading Israel to victory in battle against the king's forces (3:26–30). **left-handed:** Evidently a common trait among ancient Benjaminites (20:16). Ironically, the name

"Benjamin" means "son of the right hand" (Gen 35:18). **tribute:** Probably in the form of produce from Israelite farms and vineyards.

3:16 cubit: Exact length uncertain but shorter than the standard cubit of 18 inches, making the weapon an optimal size for concealment. **right thigh:** Helps to explain how the weapon slipped past the royal security, since short swords were typically strapped to the left leg.

3:19 sculptured stones: Idol images associated with a shrine that seems to have stood on the west bank of the Jordan. **I have a secret message:** A request for a private audience.

3:22 dirt came out: Feces is expelled from the wound.

3:26 Seirah: In the hill country of Ephraim, but exact location unknown.

3:27 the trumpet: Blown to muster the Israelites for war. For background, see word study: *Trumpet* at 6:34. **Ephraim:** The tribal territory in central Palestine.

3:30 eighty years: The longest period of respite achieved in Judges.

c The meaning of the Hebrew word is unknown.

Victories of the Judges

Oppressor	Oppression	Deliverer	Era of Peace	Verses
Mesopotamia	8 years	Othniel	40 years	Judg 3:7–11
Moabites	18 years	Ehud	80 years	Judg 3:12–30
Philistines	?	Shamgar	?	Judg 3:31
Canaanites	20 years	Deborah	40 years	Judg 4:1—5:31
Midianites	7 years	Gideon	40 years	Judg 6:1—8:32
Abimelech	3 years	Tola, Jair	45 years	Judg 8:33—10:5
Ammonites	18 years	Jephthah, Ibzan, Elon, Abdon	6, 7, 10, 8 yrs.	Judg 10:6—12:15
Philistines	40 years	Samson	20 years	Judg 13:1—16:31

the hand of Israel. And the land had rest for eighty years.

Shamgar

31 After him was Shamgar the son of A'nath, who killed six hundred of the Philis'tines with an oxgoad; and he too delivered Israel.

Deborah and Barak

4 And the sons of Israel again did what was evil in the sight of the Lord, after E'hud died. ²And the Lord sold them into the hand of Ja'bin king of Canaan, who reigned in Ha'zor; the commander of his army was Sis'era, who dwelt in Haro'sheth-ha-goi'im. ³Then the sons of Israel cried to the Lord for help; for he had nine hundred chariots of iron, and oppressed the sons of Israel cruelly for twenty years.

4 Now Deborah, a prophetess, the wife of Lap'pidoth, was judging Israel at that time. ⁵She used to sit under the palm of Deborah between Ra'mah and Bethel in the hill country of E'phraim; and the sons of Israel came up to her for judgment. ⁶She sent and summoned Barak the son of Abin'o-am from Ke'desh in Naph'tali, and said to him, "The Lord, the God of Israel, commands you, 'Go, gather your men at Mount Ta'bor, taking ten thousand from the tribe of Naphtali and the tribe of Zeb'ulun. ⁷And I will draw out Sis'era, the general of Ja'bin's army, to meet you by the river Ki'shon with his chariots and his troops; and I will give him into your hand.'" ⁸Barak said to her, "If you will go with me, I will go; but if you will not go with me, I will not go." ⁹And she said, "I will surely go with you; nevertheless, the road on which you are going will not lead to your glory, for the Lord will sell Sis'era into the hand of a woman." Then Deborah arose, and went with Barak to Ke'desh. ¹⁰And Barak summoned Zeb'ulun and Naph'tali to Ke'desh; and ten thousand men went up at his heels; and Deborah went up with him.

11 Now He'ber the Kenite had separated from the Kenites, the descendants of Ho'bab the father-in-law of Moses, and had pitched his tent as far away as the oak in Za-anan'nim, which is near Ke'desh.

12 When Sis'era was told that Barak the son of Abin'o-am had gone up to Mount Ta'bor, ¹³Sis'era called out all his chariots, nine hundred chariots of iron, and all the men who were with him, from Haro'sheth-ha-goi'im to the river Ki'shon. ¹⁴And Deborah said to Barak, "Up! For this is the day in which the Lord has given Sis'era into your hand. Does not the Lord go out before you?" So Barak

---

3:31 Shamgar: Nothing is known of him beyond this verse, although brief mention is again made of him in 5:6. **son of Anath:** Since Anath is the name of a Semitic goddess of warfare, many surmise that Shamgar was not an Israelite. His mother appears to have come from a Canaanite family, and no tribal affiliation is given to inform us about his father. **Philistines:** Newcomers to southwest Canaan in the period of the judges. See note on 3:3. **oxgoad:** A sharpened implement used to prod cattle and discourage them from kicking back at the plowman. Shamgar's success in wielding this unconventional weapon anticipates the story of Samson clubbing down the Philistines with a donkey's jawbone (15:15–17).

4:1–5:31 The story of Deborah and Barak. Judges 4 is a prose account of Israel's victory over northern Canaanite oppressors, and Judges 5 is a poetic account of the same triumph. Two women, Deborah and Jael, stand out in these episodes for their heroic actions, showing that women have an integral role to play in the economy of salvation (CCC 489).

4:2 Jabin: Probably a dynastic title rather than a personal name, since an earlier king with the same name appears in Hazor in Josh 11:1. **king of Canaan:** The most prominent king in northern Canaan. He may have formed an alliance with other monarchs in the region (the "kings" of 5:19). **Hazor:** A Canaanite stronghold in upper Galilee. See note on Josh 11:1. **Sisera:** A non-Semitic name, perhaps indicating he was one of the Sea Peoples who migrated to the Near East during the time of the judges. **Harosheth:** Southeast of Mount Carmel.

4:3 chariots of iron: Military technology unmatched in early Israel. See note on 1:19.

4:4 Deborah: Her name means "honey bee". Unlike most women in biblical times, she holds positions of civil authority (local magistrate, 4:5) and religious influence (prophetess, 4:6). She is affectionately remembered as "a mother in Israel" (5:7). Deborah hails from the tribe of Ephraim and is the only major judge whose death is not recorded in the book (CCC 489). • Deborah stands alongside other prominent figures of the Bible who perform judicial as well as prophetic functions. Moses was a judge and a prophet before her (Ex 18:13; Deut 34:10), and Samuel will fulfill these same roles after her (1 Sam 3:20; 7:15–17). Scripture knows of several other women who serve the Lord as prophetesses (Ex 15:20; 2 Kings 22:14; Lk 2:36; Acts 21:8–9). **Lappidoth:** His name means "torches".

4:5 sit: A sign of presiding with authority (Ex 18:13). **palm of Deborah:** About ten miles north of Jerusalem, but the exact location is unknown.

4:6 Barak: His name means "lightning". He is a military commander of northern Israelite forces. Although reluctant to mobilize Israel's volunteer militia for war unless accompanied by Deborah (4:8), he leads his troops to victory and is later noted for his faith (Heb 11:32–34). **Kedesh:** About 17 miles north of the Sea of Galilee in the tribal territory of Naphtali. **Mount Tabor:** A conspicuous peak in lower Galilee, selected as a staging point for the battle.

4:7 the river Kishon: Flows northwest across the Plain of Megiddo and empties into the Mediterranean Sea. It is fed by streams from the Galilean hills and Mount Gilboa.

4:8 If you will go with me: Barak's hesitation is a momentary act of disobedience to the word of God delivered through the prophetess (4:6–7). Consequently, the honor of victory will go to an unknown woman (Jael) instead of Barak, who should have epitomized manly bravery (4:9).

4:9 Kedesh: Not the town mentioned in 4:6, but another in the vicinity of Mount Tabor.

4:10 Zebulun and Naphtali: Both tribes heed the summons to battle (5:18). Four other tribes rally behind Barak according to the poetic account in 5:14–15 (Ephraim, Benjamin, Manasseh, and Issachar).

4:11 separated: Heber breaks away from the Kenites living in southern Canaan and settles his family in northern Canaan. See note on 1:16. **Hobab:** Here called the father-in-law of Moses, but elsewhere called the brother-in-law of Moses (Num 10:29). The discrepancy is likely a matter of vocalization: the Hebrew term for "father-in-law" (*hoten*) has the same consonants as "brother-in-law" (*hatan*), and since Hebrew was originally written without vowels, it seems that the latter was misread as the former. On this solution, Hobab is not the father of Moses' wife, Zipporah, but her brother.

went down from Mount Ta'bor with ten thousand men following him. ¹⁵And the Lord routed Sis'era and all his chariots and all his army before Barak at the edge of the sword; and Sisera alighted from his chariot and fled away on foot. ¹⁶And Barak pursued the chariots and the army to Haro'sheth-ha-goi'im, and all the army of Sis'era fell by the edge of the sword; not a man was left.

Jael Kills Sisera

17 But Sis'era fled away on foot to the tent of Ja'el, the wife of He'ber the Kenite; for there was peace between Ja'bin the king of Ha'zor and the house of Heber the Kenite. ¹⁸And Ja'el came out to meet Sis'era, and said to him, "Turn aside, my lord, turn aside to me; have no fear." So he turned aside to her into the tent, and she covered him with a rug. ¹⁹And he said to her, "Please, give me a little water to drink; for I am thirsty." So she opened a skin of milk and gave him a drink and covered him. ²⁰And he said to her, "Stand at the door of the tent, and if any man comes and asks you, 'Is any one here?' say, No." ²¹But Ja'el the wife of He'ber took a tent peg, and took a hammer in her hand, and went softly to him and drove the peg into his temple, till it went down into the ground, as he was lying fast asleep from weariness. So he died. ²²And behold, as Barak pursued Sis'era, Ja'el went out to meet him, and said to him, "Come, and I will show you the man whom you are seeking." So he went in to her tent; and there lay Sisera dead, with the tent peg in his temple.

23 So on that day God subdued Ja'bin the king of Canaan before the sons of Israel. ²⁴And the hand of the sons of Israel bore harder and harder on Ja'bin

the king of Canaan, until they destroyed Jabin king of Canaan.

The Song of Deborah

5 Then sang Deborah and Barak the son of Abin'o-am on that day:*
²"That the leaders took the lead in Israel,
    that the people offered themselves willingly,
    bless**ᵈ** the Lord!

³"Hear, O kings; give ear, O princes;
    to the Lord I will sing,
    I will make melody to the Lord, the God of Israel.

⁴"Lord, when you went forth from Se'ir,
    when you marched from the region of E'dom,
the earth trembled,
    and the heavens dropped,
    yes, the clouds dropped water.
⁵The mountains quaked before the Lord,
    the One of Sinai, before the Lord, the God of Israel.

⁶"In the days of Shamgar, son of A'nath,
    in the days of Ja'el, caravans ceased
    and travelers kept to the byways.
⁷The peasantry ceased in Israel, they ceased
    until you arose, Deborah,
    arose as a mother in Israel.
⁸When new gods were chosen,
    then war was in the gates.
Was shield or spear to be seen
    among forty thousand in Israel?

4:15 routed: The poetic version in 5:20-21 indicates the Lord sends a powerful rainstorm to flood the Kishon and immobilize the Canaanite chariot corps, which would otherwise have a tactical advantage on the level plain. The event recalls Yahweh's victory over the Egyptian chariots at the Red Sea (Ex 14:24-25).

4:17 Jael: Her name means "mountain goat". She may be a Kenite like her husband, Heber; alternatively, she may be an Israelite who has married into a Kenite family, as this would better explain her hostility toward Sisera (4:21), despite the **peace** between the breakaway group of northern Kenites and the local Canaanites. Either way, the Lord blesses her (5:24) and uses her to fight for the side of Israel (4:9).

🕮 **4:21 drove:** The same verb appeared in 3:21 (Heb., *taqa'*) to describe Ehud thrusting his sword into Eglon. **So he died:** It was considered humiliating for a man to be slain by a woman (9:53-54). • *Allegorically,* the woman Jael is a figure of the Church. Ascending from earthly to heavenly things she kills Sisera, symbolic of fleshly vices, with a stake. That is, she brings him down by the power of the wood of the Cross (Origen of Alexandria, *Homilies on Judges* 5, 5).

5:1-31 The Song of Deborah, a victory hymn that celebrates Israel's triumph over hostile Canaanites with the help

of the Lord (4:15). It is a classic specimen of early Hebrew poetry that many believe was composed soon after the events it commemorates, i.e., in the latter half of the second millennium B.C. Several lines are difficult to decipher, partly because the language of the poem is archaic and partly because the text seems to have suffered a degree of corruption during the process of transmission. For similar commemorative songs, see the Song at the Sea (Ex 15:1-18) and the Song of Heshbon (Num 21:27-30).

5:2 That the leaders ... Israel: Meaning obscure. The text is literally: "When hair was loose in Israel", perhaps a reference to persons consecrated by a Nazirite vow (Num 6:5).

5:4 Seir: The hill country of Edom, south of the Dead Sea. From here Yahweh, the divine Warrior, marches east of the Jordan and leads Israel into Canaan (Num 20:14—21:35). **earth trembled ... clouds dropped water:** Frightful displays of divine power, reminiscent of the Sinai theophany, where God revealed himself to Israel in a mighty earthquake and violent thunderstorm (Ex 19:16-18). This serves as a prelude to Yahweh's dramatic interventions on behalf of Israel in battling the Canaanites.

5:6 Shamgar: Introduced in 3:31. **Jael:** See note on 4:17.

5:7 Deborah: See note on 4:4.

5:8 new gods were chosen: By Israelites who forsook the Lord and worshiped the pagan deities of Canaan. Idolatry provokes the anger of Yahweh and brings the punishment of war upon his people (2:11-14; 3:7-8, etc.). **shield or spear:** Weapons wielded by professional soldiers. These are not found among the militiamen of Israel (1 Sam 13:22).

ᵈOr *You who offered yourselves willingly among the people, bless.*
* 5:1: The song of Deborah gives an alternative to the prose account of the previous chapter. Though touched up by later editors, it is very ancient and gives a valuable picture of the state of Israel in the thirteenth century B.C.

⁹My heart goes out to the commanders of Israel
  who offered themselves willingly among the
    people.
  Bless the Lord.

¹⁰"Tell of it, you who ride on tawny donkeys,
  you who sit on rich carpets ᵉ
  and you who walk by the way.
¹¹To the sound of musicians ᵉ at the watering
    places,
  there they repeat the triumphs of the Lord,
  the triumphs of his peasantry in Israel.

  "Then down to the gates marched
    the people of the Lord.
¹²"Awake, awake, Deborah!
  Awake, awake, utter a song!
  Arise, Barak, lead away your captives,
  O son of Abin'o-am.
¹³Then down marched the remnant of the noble;
  the people of the Lord marched down for him ᶠ
    against the mighty.
¹⁴From E'phraim they set out there ˣ into the
    valley, ᵍ
  following you, Benjamin, with your kinsmen;
  from Ma'chir marched down the commanders,
    and from Zeb'ulun those who bear the
    marshal's staff;
¹⁵the princes of Is'sachar came with Deborah,
  and Issachar faithful to Barak;
  into the valley they rushed forth at his heels.
  Among the clans of Reuben
    there were great searchings of heart.
¹⁶Why did you tarry among the sheepfolds,
  to hear the piping for the flocks?

Among the clans of Reuben
  there were great searchings of heart.
¹⁷Gilead stayed beyond the Jordan;
  and Dan, why did he abide with the ships?
  Asher sat still at the coast of the sea,
    settling down by his landings.
¹⁸Zeb'ulun is a people that jeoparded their lives to
    the death;
  Naph'tali too, on the heights of the field.

¹⁹"The kings came, they fought;
  then fought the kings of Canaan,
  at Ta'anach, by the waters of Megid'do;
    they got no spoils of silver.
²⁰From heaven fought the stars,
  from their courses they fought against Sis'era.
²¹The torrent Ki'shon swept them away,
  the onrushing torrent, the torrent Kishon.
  March on, my soul, with might!

²²"Then loud beat the horses' hoofs
  with the galloping, galloping of his steeds.

²³"Curse Me'roz, says the angel of the Lord,
  curse bitterly its inhabitants,
  because they came not to the help of the Lord,
    to the help of the Lord against the mighty.

²⁴"Most blessed of women be Ja'el,
  the wife of He'ber the Kenite,
  of tent-dwelling women most blessed.
²⁵He asked for water and she gave him milk,
  she brought him curds in a lordly bowl.
²⁶She put her hand to the tent peg
  and her right hand to the workmen's mallet;

5:10 you who ride: Wealthy nobles. **you who walk:** The general population.

5:13 marched down: The armies of Israel rush down the slopes of Mount Tabor to the battlefield below (4:14).

5:14–18 The wartime response of Israel is assessed. Six tribes are praised for risking their lives and supporting the war effort (Ephraim, Benjamin, Manasseh, Zebulun, Issachar, Naphtali), while four tribes are rebuked for staying home and exempting themselves from the conflict (Reuben, Gad, Dan, Asher). Two tribes, Judah and Simeon, are unmentioned because they occupy southern Canaan and are probably unaffected by the Canaanite tyranny up north. The poem makes it clear that Israel, once united in the days of Joshua, is becoming divided in the days of the judges.

5:14 Machir: A prominent clan of the tribe of Manasseh, named after the firstborn son of Manasseh the patriarch (Num 26:29; Josh 17:1).

5:17 Gilead: The tribal territory of Gad, east of the Jordan (Josh 13:24–25). **with the ships:** Dan is allotted a portion of western coastland as its home (Josh 19:40–46), but eventually the tribe migrates to northern Israel (18:1–31).

5:19 waters of Megiddo: The Kishon River and its tributaries that flow through the fertile Plain of Megiddo (4:7). Overlooking the plain is the fortified town of Megiddo, which was the site of several important battles in biblical times (e.g., 2 Chron 35:20–25).

5:20 the stars: Heavenly powers under the command of Yahweh fight for Israel on earth (cf. Josh 5:13–15). The next verse (5:21) suggests they bring torrential rains that cause flash flooding on the day of battle. Stars were believed to represent angels in biblical times (Job 38:7; Dan 8:10; Rev 1:20).

5:21 onrushing torrent: Apparently the river Kishon overflows its banks and floods the battlefield. In this way, the Lord, who wields creation as his weapon, disables the Canaanite chariots. For similar acts of divine warfare, see Ex 14:24–28 and Josh 10:11.

5:23 Meroz: A town of unknown location that refuses the summons to battle.

5:24 Most blessed: Extraordinary praise for an otherwise ordinary woman. • Similar words will be spoken to the heroine Judith after she severs the head of General Holofernes in a tent (Jud 13:18) and then to Mary, the mother of Jesus, when she plays an instrumental role with her Son in trampling the head of the Satanic deceiver (Lk 1:42; cf. Gen 3:15) (CCC 489).

5:26 crushed his head: See the similar event in 9:53, where a woman crushes the skull of the wicked Abimelech.

ᵉ The meaning of the Hebrew word is uncertain.
ᶠ Gk: Heb *me*.
ˣ Cn: Heb *From Ephraim their root.*
ᵍ Gk: Heb *in Amalek.*

she struck Sis'era a blow,
  she crushed his head,
    she shattered and pierced his temple.
²⁷He sank, he fell,
  he lay still at her feet;
at her feet he sank, he fell;
  where he sank, there he fell dead.

²⁸"Out of the window she peered,
  the mother of Sis'era gazed ^h through the
    lattice:
'Why is his chariot so long in coming?
  Why do the hoofbeats of his chariots tarry?'
²⁹Her wisest ladies make answer,
  no, she gives answer to herself,
³⁰'Are they not finding and dividing the spoil?—
  A maiden or two for every man;
spoil of dyed stuffs for Sis'era,
  spoil of dyed stuffs embroidered,
    two pieces of dyed work embroidered for my
      neck as spoil?'

³¹"So perish all your enemies, O Lord!
  But your friends be like the sun as he rises in
    his might."

And the land had rest for forty years.

The Midianite Oppression

6 The sons of Israel did what was evil in the sight of the Lord; and the Lord gave them into the hand of Mid'ian seven years. ²And the hand of Mid'ian prevailed over Israel; and because of Midian the sons of Israel made for themselves the dens which are in the mountains, and the caves and the strongholds. ³For whenever the Israelites put in seed the Mid'ianites and the Amal'ekites and the people of the East would come up and attack them; ⁴they would encamp against them and destroy the produce of the land, as far as the neighborhood of Gaza, and leave no sustenance in Israel, and no sheep or ox or donkey. ⁵For they would come up with their cattle and their tents, coming like locusts for number; both they and their camels could not be counted; so that they wasted the land as they came in. ⁶And Israel was brought very low because of Mid'ian; and the sons of Israel cried for help to the Lord.

7 When the sons of Israel cried to the Lord on account of the Mid'ianites, ⁸the Lord sent a prophet to the sons of Israel; and he said to them, "Thus says the Lord, the God of Israel: I led you up from Egypt, and brought you out of the house of bondage; ⁹and I delivered you from the hand of the Egyptians, and from the hand of all who oppressed you, and drove them out before you, and gave you their land; ¹⁰and I said to you, 'I am the Lord your God; you shall not pay reverence to the gods of the Am'orites, in whose land you dwell.' But you have not given heed to my voice."

The Call of Gideon

11 Now the angel of the Lord came and sat under the oak at Oph'rah, which belonged to Jo'ash the Abiez'rite, as his son Gideon was beating out wheat in the wine press, to hide it from the Mid'ianites.

5:31: Rev 1:16.

5:28–30 A moving but tragic portrayal of Sisera's mother growing anxious over her son's delayed return from battle.

5:31 your friends: Literally, "those who love him [= Yahweh]". **like the sun:** A prayer for Israel to grow stronger and stronger, just as the rising sun grows brighter and warmer as dawn gives way to full daylight. • Scripture teaches that the saints are destined to "shine like the sun" (Mt 13:43), just as Jesus radiates God's glory on the mount of Transfiguration (Mt 17:2) and continues to do so in heaven (Rev 1:16).

6:1–8:35 The judgeship of Gideon, also called Jerubaal (6:32). He is a deliverer from the tribe of Manasseh (6:15) whose name means "one who hacks/cuts down". Central to the account is the question of kingship. Gideon upholds the theocratic ideal that Yahweh's rule as King over Israel is sufficient for the nation's security and prosperity (8:23). The people, however, desire an earthly king and propose that Gideon assume the office (8:22).

6:1 Midian: In northwest Arabia. The hostility of the Midianites toward Israel goes back to the wilderness period (Num 22:1–7). Genesis traces the ancestral origin of the Midianites to Abraham through his second wife, Keturah (Gen 25:1–2).

6:3 Amalekites: A nomadic people from the Sinai Peninsula, hostile to Israel since the time of the Exodus (Ex 17:8–16). **people of the East:** Invaders from northern Arabia.

6:5 like locusts: Suggests that the desert marauders are numerous, like the locust hoards feared by Near Eastern farmers, and that they rove the countryside destroying fields and food supplies, just like their insect counterparts. No other account in Judges presents such a full description of the oppression that weighs upon Israel.

6:8 prophet: Unnamed and unknown, beyond the fact that he exposes idolatry as the cause of Israel's hardships (6:10). The implied lesson: the sooner God's people repent, the sooner their troubles will cease.

6:10 gods of the Amorites: The pagan deities worshiped in Canaan.

6:11–24 The call of Gideon. • Several parallels with the call of Moses at the burning bush are noticeable: **(1)** both receive their call from the angel of the Lord (6:12; Ex 3:2); **(2)** both are sent to deliver Israel from enemy oppression (6:14; Ex 3:7–10); **(3)** both are reluctant to accept the mission and raise objections about being unqualified and insufficient for the task (6:15; Ex 3:11; 4:1, 10); **(4)** both are assured that the Lord will be with them (6:16; Ex 3:12); and **(5)** both callings are confirmed by miraculous signs (6:17–22, 36–40; Ex 3:12; 4:2–9).

6:11 angel of the Lord: A divine messenger who speaks and acts in the name of Yahweh. The closeness between the two is evident in the story, for this heavenly figure is also called "the angel of God" (6:20) and even "the Lord" (6:14, 16, 23) (CCC 332). See word study: *Angel of the Lord* at Gen 16:7. **Ophrah:** Location uncertain, but probably in the Jezreel valley, southwest of the Sea of Galilee. **beating ... wheat:** Normally done on an elevated threshing floor, exposed to the wind.

---

^hGk Compare Tg: Heb *exclaimed*.

¹²And the angel of the LORD appeared to him and said to him, "The LORD is with you, you mighty man of valor." ¹³And Gideon said to him, "Please, sir, if the LORD is with us, why then has all this befallen us? And where are all his wonderful deeds which our fathers recounted to us, saying, 'Did not the LORD bring us up from Egypt?' But now the LORD has cast us off, and given us into the hand of Mid'ian." ¹⁴And the LORD turned to him and said, "Go in this might of yours and deliver Israel from the hand of Mid'ian; do not I send you?" ¹⁵And he said to him, "Please, Lord, how can I deliver Israel? Behold, my clan is the weakest in Manas'seh, and I am the least in my family." ¹⁶And the LORD said to him, "But I will be with you, and you shall strike the Mid'ianites as one man." ¹⁷And he said to him, "If now I have found favor with you, then show me a sign that it is you who speak with me. ¹⁸Do not depart from here, I beg you, until I come to you, and bring out my present, and set it before you." And he said, "I will stay till you return."

19 So Gideon went into his house and prepared a kid, and unleavened cakes from an ephah of flour; the meat he put in a basket, and the broth he put in a pot, and brought them to him under the oak and presented them. ²⁰And the angel of God said to him, "Take the meat and the unleavened cakes, and put them on this rock, and pour the broth over them." And he did so. ²¹Then the angel of the LORD reached out the tip of the staff that was in his hand, and touched the meat and the unleavened cakes; and there sprang up fire from the rock and consumed the flesh and the unleavened cakes; and the angel of the LORD vanished from his sight. ²²Then Gideon perceived that he was the angel of the LORD; and Gideon said, "Alas, O Lord GOD! For now I have

seen the angel of the LORD face to face." ²³But the LORD said to him, "Peace be to you; do not fear, you shall not die." ²⁴Then Gideon built an altar there to the LORD, and called it, The LORD is peace. To this day it still stands at Oph'rah, which belongs to the Abiez'rites.

25 That night the LORD said to him, "Take your father's bull, the second bull seven years old, and pull down the altar of Ba'al which your father has, and cut down the Ashe'rah that is beside it; ²⁶and build an altar to the LORD your God on the top of the stronghold here, with stones laid in due order; then take the second bull, and offer it as a burnt offering with the wood of the Ashe'rah which you shall cut down." ²⁷So Gideon took ten men of his servants, and did as the LORD had told him; but because he was too afraid of his family and the men of the town to do it by day, he did it by night.

Gideon Destroys the Altar of Baal

28 When the men of the town rose early in the morning, behold, the altar of Ba'al was broken down, and the Ashe'rah beside it was cut down, and the second bull was offered upon the altar which had been built. ²⁹And they said to one another, "Who has done this thing?" And after they had made search and inquired, they said, "Gideon the son of Jo'ash has done this thing." ³⁰Then the men of the town said to Jo'ash, "Bring out your son, that he may die, for he has pulled down the altar of Ba'al and cut down the Ashe'rah beside it." ³¹But Jo'ash said to all who were arrayed against him, "Will you contend for Ba'al? Or will you defend his cause? Whoever contends for him shall be put to death by morning. If he is a god, let him contend for himself, because his altar has been pulled down." ³²Therefore on that

---

6:15 I am the least: God often chooses the weak of the world to bring down the strong, so that none should boast of the triumph as his own doing (1 Cor 1:26–29). This principle is clearly illustrated in the Gideon story (7:2–3).

6:19 kid ... cakes: Brings to mind how Abraham entertained heavenly guests with meat and bread under the shade of a tree (Gen 18:1–8).

6:21 consumed: A sign that God accepts the offering, as in Lev 9:24. • *Allegorically*, the rock is Christ, and his crucified flesh, filled with the divine Spirit, burns away both the kid of our sinful deeds and the broth of our sinful desires (St. Ambrose, *The Holy Spirit* 1, 3).

6:22 face to face: Gazing upon God with mortal eyes is feared as something dangerous and even deadly (13:22; Gen 16:13; 32:30).

6:25 pull down: Demolition of Canaanite worship sites and cultic apparatus are mandated by the Mosaic Law (Ex 34:13; Deut 7:5). **Baal:** Canaanite god of fertility. See note on 2:11. **Asherah:** Canaanite goddess represented as a tree or wooden pole (Ex 34:13; Deut 16:21).

6:26 an altar: A platform made of stacked, undressed stones (Ex 20:25). **burnt offering:** A sacrifice wholly consumed by the fires of the altar.

6:32 Jerubaal: Means "let Baal contend" and recalls the appeal of Joash to let Baal avenge himself against Gideon for attacking the deity's honor.

WORD STUDY

Trumpet (6:34)

shophar (Heb.): A curved ram's horn used as a trumpet. Among its uses, the hollow ram's horn is blown to signal the start of a Jubilee year (Lev 25:9), to announce the coronation of a new king (1 Kings 1:34), and to give warning that the judgment of God is coming (Zeph 1:16). Its most frequent uses, however, are for worship and warfare. On the one hand, the trumpet is a liturgical instrument used to assemble the faithful before God (Joel 2:15) and to praise the Lord in worshipful music and procession (2 Sam 6:15; Ps 150:3). On the other, the trumpet is a military instrument used to mobilize tribal fighters for war (Judg 3:27; 6:34), to initiate their engagement in battle (Judg 7:22), and to halt the advance of an army when the opposition flees (2 Sam 2:28; 18:16). Occasionally both aspects are combined, as at the siege of Jericho, when the priests of Israel use trumpets to lead the sacred procession around the city and to initiate the attack on its inhabitants (Josh 6:4–9, 20).

day he was called Jerubba'al, that is to say, "Let Ba'al contend against him," because he pulled down his altar.

33 Then all the Mid'ianites and the Amal'ekites and the people of the East came together, and crossing the Jordan they encamped in the Valley of Jezre'el. [34]But the Spirit of the LORD took possession of Gideon; and he sounded the trumpet, and the Abiez'rites were called out to follow him. [35]And he sent messengers throughout all Manas'seh; and they too were called out to follow him. And he sent messengers to Asher, Zeb'ulun, and Naph'tali; and they went up to meet them.

The Sign of the Fleece

36 Then Gideon said to God, "If you will deliver Israel by my hand, as you have said, [37]behold, I am laying a fleece of wool on the threshing floor; if there is dew on the fleece alone, and it is dry on all the ground, then I shall know that you will deliver Israel by my hand, as you have said." [38]And it was so. When he rose early next morning and squeezed the fleece, he wrung enough dew from the fleece to fill a bowl with water. [39]Then Gideon said to God, "Let not your anger burn against me, let me speak but this once; please, let me make trial only this once with the fleece; please, let it be dry only on the fleece, and on all the ground let there be dew." [40]And God did so that night; for it was dry on the fleece only, and on all the ground there was dew.

Gideon's Army Selected

7 Then Jerubba'al (that is, Gideon) and all the people who were with him rose early and encamped beside the spring of Harod; and the camp of Mid'ian was north of them, by the hill of Mo'reh, in the valley.

2 The LORD said to Gideon, "The people with you are too many for me to give the Mid'ianites into their hand, lest Israel vaunt themselves against me, saying, 'My own hand has delivered me.' [3]Now therefore proclaim in the ears of the people, saying,

'Whoever is fearful and trembling, let him return home.'" And Gideon tested them;[i] twenty-two thousand returned, and ten thousand remained.

4 And the LORD said to Gideon, "The people are still too many; take them down to the water and I will test them for you there; and he of whom I say to you, 'This man shall go with you,' shall go with you; and any of whom I say to you, 'This man shall not go with you,' shall not go." [5]So he brought the people down to the water; and the LORD said to Gideon, "Every one that laps the water with his tongue, as a dog laps, you shall set by himself; likewise every one that kneels down to drink." [6]And the number of those that lapped, putting their hands to their mouths, was three hundred men; but all the rest of the people knelt down to drink water. [7]And the LORD said to Gideon, "With the three hundred men that lapped I will deliver you and give the Mid'ianites into your hand; and let all the others go every man to his home." [8]So he took the jars of the people from their hands,[j] and their trumpets; and he sent all the rest of Israel every man to his tent, but retained the three hundred men; and the camp of Mid'ian was below him in the valley.

Gideon Routs the Midianites

9 That same night the LORD said to him, "Arise, go down against the camp; for I have given it into your hand. [10]But if you fear to go down, go down to the camp with Pu'rah your servant; [11]and you shall hear what they say, and afterward your hands shall be strengthened to go down against the camp." Then he went down with Pu'rah his servant to the outposts of the armed men that were in the camp. [12]And the Mid'ianites and the Amal'ekites and all the people of the East lay along the valley like locusts for multitude; and their camels were without number, as the sand which is upon the seashore for multitude. [13]When Gideon came, behold, a man was telling a dream to his comrade; and he said, "Behold, I dreamed a dream; and a cake of barley

---

6:33 Valley of Jezreel: The fertile plain southwest of the Sea of Galilee.

6:34 took possession: Literally, the Spirit "clothed" Gideon with his power and authority. The same language is used elsewhere in the Bible in 1 Chron 12:18, 2 Chron 24:20, and Lk 24:49. See note on 3:10.

6:36–40 Gideon presses the Lord for two additional signs to confirm his mission.

✠ **6:38 squeezed the fleece:** Wringing dew out of fleece was a technique used in places where a natural water supply was either insufficient or entirely lacking. • *Allegorically*, the dew on the fleece is the faith that first came to Israel, while the world all around was dry, but later it came to moisten the Gentiles. *Morally*, the miracle was performed on a threshing floor as a sign of the harvest of virtues that come through faith (St. Ambrose, *The Holy Spirit* 1, 6–10).

7:1–25 Gideon routs the Midianites and their allies. At the Lord's prompting, he downsizes his army (7:1–8), gathers pre-

war intelligence (7:9–14), stages a surprise nighttime attack (7:15–16), and chases the enemy out of Canaan (7:19–25).

7:1 spring of Harod: Near the foothills of Mount Gilboa, just south of the Jezreel valley.

7:2 too many: Gideon must scale back his army of 32,000 soldiers (7:3) to a mere 300 men (7:7). Weakening his forces so drastically is meant to encourage faith in Yahweh's power and to discourage pride in human strength and tactical wisdom. Once again, Israel learns that the battle belongs to the Lord and that victory in war is the work of divine might.

7:3 fearful and trembling: Conditions that qualify for a combat exemption (Deut 20:8).

7:6 lapped: Implies the men are still on their feet, standing ready and alert.

7:10 servant: Purah is a personal attendant, possibly Gideon's armor bearer (the same Hebrew term is rendered "young man" in 9:54 and 1 Sam 14:1).

7:13 a dream: Envisions the farmers of Israel (**barley bread**) prevailing over the nomadic peoples of Midian (**tent**). For dreams as channels of divine revelation, see word study: *Dream* at Gen 37:5.

---

[i] Cn: Heb *and depart from Mount Gilead.*
[j] Cn: Heb *the people took provisions in their hands.*

bread tumbled into the camp of Mid'ian, and came to the tent, and struck it so that it fell, and turned it upside down, so that the tent lay flat." ¹⁴And his comrade answered, "This is no other than the sword of Gideon the son of Jo'ash, a man of Israel; into his hand God has given Mid'ian and all the host."

15 When Gideon heard the telling of the dream and its interpretation, he worshiped; and he returned to the camp of Israel, and said, "Arise; for the LORD has given the host of Mid'ian into your hand." ¹⁶And he divided the three hundred men into three companies, and put trumpets into the hands of all of them and empty jars, with torches inside the jars. ¹⁷And he said to them, "Look at me, and do likewise; when I come to the outskirts of the camp, do as I do. ¹⁸When I blow the trumpet, I and all who are with me, then blow the trumpets also on every side of all the camp, and shout, 'For the LORD and for Gideon.'"

19 So Gideon and the hundred men who were with him came to the outskirts of the camp at the beginning of the middle watch, when they had just set the watch; and they blew the trumpets and smashed the jars that were in their hands. ²⁰And the three companies blew the trumpets and broke the jars, holding in their left hands the torches, and in their right hands the trumpets to blow; and they cried, "A sword for the LORD and for Gideon!" ²¹They stood every man in his place round about the camp, and all the army ran; they cried out and fled. ²²When they blew the three hundred trumpets, the LORD set every man's sword against his fellow and against all the army; and the army fled as far as Beth-shit'tah toward Zer'erah,ᵏ as far as the border of Abel-meho'lah, by Tabbath. ²³And the men of Israel were called out from Naph'tali and from Asher and from all Manas'seh, and they pursued after Mid'ian.

24 And Gideon sent messengers throughout all the hill country of E'phraim, saying, "Come down against the Mid'ianites and seize the waters against them, as far as Beth-bar'ah, and also the Jordan." So all the men of Ephraim were called out, and they seized the waters as far as Beth-barah, and also the Jordan. ²⁵And they took the two princes of Mid'ian,

Or'eb and Ze'eb; they killed Oreb at the rock of Oreb, and Zeeb they killed at the wine press of Zeeb, as they pursued Midian; and they brought the heads of Oreb and Zeeb to Gideon beyond the Jordan.

Gideon's Triumph

8 And the men of E'phraim said to him, "What is this that you have done to us, not to call us when you went to fight with Mid'ian?" And they upbraided him violently. ²And he said to them, "What have I done now in comparison with you? Is not the gleaning of the grapes of E'phraim better than the vintage of Abie'zer? ³God has given into your hands the princes of Mid'ian, Or'eb and Ze'eb; what have I been able to do in comparison with you?" Then their anger against him was abated, when he had said this.

4 And Gideon came to the Jordan and passed over, he and the three hundred men who were with him, faint yet pursuing. ⁵So he said to the men of Succoth, "Please, give loaves of bread to the people who follow me; for they are faint, and I am pursuing after Zebah and Zalmun'na, the kings of Mid'ian." ⁶And the officials of Succoth said, "Are Zebah and Zalmun'na already in your hand, that we should give bread to your army?" ⁷And Gideon said, "Well then, when the LORD has given Zebah and Zalmun'na into my hand, I will flail your flesh with the thorns of the wilderness and with briers." ⁸And from there he went up to Penu'el, and spoke to them in the same way; and the men of Penuel answered him as the men of Succoth had answered. ⁹And he said to the men of Penu'el, "When I come again in peace, I will break down this tower."

10 Now Zebah and Zalmun'na were in Karkor with their army, about fifteen thousand men, all who were left of all the army of the people of the East; for there had fallen a hundred and twenty thousand men who drew the sword. ¹¹And Gideon went up by the caravan route east of No'bah and Jog'behah, and attacked the army; for the army was off its guard. ¹²And Zebah and Zalmun'na fled; and he pursued them and took the two kings of Mid'ian, Zebah and Zalmunna, and he threw all the army into a panic.

7:15 he worshiped: A fitting prelude to the Lord's war.

7:19 middle watch: The night was divided into three watches between sundown (about 6 P.M.) and sunrise (about 6 A.M.). The middle watch began at roughly 10 P.M.

7:22 the army fled: Eastward across the Jordan River.

7:24 Ephraim: Settled in central Canaan, the tribe is called upon to cut off Midian's escape.

7:25 Oreb: Means "raven". **Zeeb:** Means "wolf".

8:2 in comparison with you: Words of kindness and praise assuage the anger of the offended Ephraimites (8:3; Prov 15:1). **the gleaning:** The unpicked grapes left behind after the vineyard has been harvested.

8:4–28 Gideon pursues the fleeing Midianites (8:4–12), slays their kings (8:18–21), and collects the spoils of war (8:22–29).

8:5 Succoth: Less than five miles east of the Jordan on the Jabbok River. It is often identified with modern Tell Deir 'Alla and lay in the tribal territory of Gad (Josh 13:27). City officials in Succoth (and then Penuel, 8:8) refuse to supply Gideon's army with provisions for fear of Midianite reprisals, should he and his men fail to win a decisive victory over the invaders (8:6). **Zebah:** Means "sacrifice". **Zalmunna:** Meaning uncertain. **kings of Midian:** Perhaps chieftains of different Midianite tribes (cf. Num 31:8).

8:8 Penuel: A few miles east of Succoth on the Jabbok River (Gen 32:31).

8:10 Karkor: Over 60 miles east of the Dead Sea. **the army:** The original force of 135,000 desert warriors is now reduced to 15,000 men. **people of the East:** Nomadic tribes from northern Arabia.

ᵏ Another reading is *Zeredah*.

13 Then Gideon the son of Jo'ash returned from the battle by the ascent of He'res. ¹⁴And he caught a young man of Succoth, and questioned him; and he wrote down for him the officials and elders of Succoth, seventy-seven men. ¹⁵And he came to the men of Succoth, and said, "Behold Zebah and Zalmun'na, about whom you taunted me, saying, 'Are Zebah and Zalmunna already in your hand, that we should give bread to your men who are faint?'" ¹⁶And he took the elders of the city and he took thorns of the wilderness and briers and with them taught the men of Succoth. ¹⁷And he broke down the tower of Penu'el, and slew the men of the city.

18 Then he said to Zebah and Zalmun'na, "Where are the men whom you slew at Ta'bor?" They answered, "As you are, so were they, every one of them; they resembled the sons of a king." ¹⁹And he said, "They were my brothers, the sons of my mother; as the LORD lives, if you had saved them alive, I would not slay you." ²⁰And he said to Je'ther his first-born, "Rise, and slay them." But the youth did not draw his sword; for he was afraid, because he was still a youth. ²¹Then Zebah and Zalmun'na said, "Rise yourself, and fall upon us; for as the man is, so is his strength." And Gideon arose and slew Zebah and Zalmunna; and he took the crescents that were on the necks of their camels.

Gideon's Ephod Becomes a Snare

22 Then the men of Israel said to Gideon, "Rule over us, you and your son and your grandson also; for you have delivered us out of the hand of Mid'ian." ²³Gideon said to them, "I will not rule over you, and my son will not rule over you; the LORD will rule over you."* ²⁴And Gideon said to them, "Let me make a request of you; give me every man of you the earrings of his spoil." (For they had golden earrings, because they were Ish'maelites.) ²⁵And they answered, "We will willingly give them." And they spread a garment, and every man cast in it the earrings of his spoil. ²⁶And the weight of the golden earrings that he requested was one thousand seven hundred shekels of gold; besides the crescents and the pendants and the purple garments worn by the kings of Mid'ian, and besides the collars that were about the necks of their camels. ²⁷And Gideon made an ephod of it and put it in his city, in Oph'rah; and all Israel played the harlot after it there, and it became a snare to Gideon and to his family. ²⁸So Mid'ian was subdued before the sons of Israel, and they lifted up their heads no more. And the land had rest forty years in the days of Gideon.

The Death of Gideon

29 Jerubba'al the son of Jo'ash went and dwelt in his own house. ³⁰Now Gideon had seventy sons, his own offspring, for he had many wives. ³¹And his concubine who was in She'chem also bore him a son, and he called his name Abim'elech. ³²And Gideon the son of Jo'ash died in a good old age, and was buried in the tomb of Jo'ash his father, at Oph'rah of the Abiez'rites.

33 As soon as Gideon died, the sons of Israel turned again and played the harlot after the Ba'als, and made Ba'al-be'rith their god. ³⁴And the sons of Israel did not remember the LORD their God, who had rescued them from the hand of all their enemies on every side; ³⁵and they did not show kindness to

---

8:13–17 Gideon makes good on his threats to punish Succoth and Penuel for refusing him help in time of need (8:7, 9). Nothing in the story indicates that Yahweh sanctioned this violence against fellow Israelites, which anticipates the more dastardly actions of Gideon's son, Abimelech (9:4–5, 42–49).

8:18 Tabor: A prominent mountain in lower Galilee (4:6).

8:19 my brothers: Gideon's male siblings were slain by the Midianites, although the event is not narrated in Judges. **as the LORD lives:** An oath formula in which Yahweh is invoked as a witness.

8:21 Rise yourself: The kings remain defiant and hurl taunting words at Gideon.

8:22–24 Impressed by his leadership in battle, the people want to make Gideon a king and the founder of a hereditary dynasty. He refuses the honor, however, because he recognizes Yahweh as the divine King of Israel (Deut 33:5) and the real Savior of his people (7:2). The outcry for an earthly king (monarchy) shows a lack of faith in the Lord's ability to rule his people effectively (theocracy). This will be made clear in 1 Sam 8:4–22, when God yields to the popular demand for royal government. Moses, endowed with prophetic foresight, had already made provision for kingship in the Torah (Deut 17:14–20).

8:24 Ishmaelites: Typically refers to the descendants of Abraham's son Ishmael, but here the term is more generic than genealogical, referring to Arabian traders (note the similar link between Ishmaelites and Midianites in Gen 37:25–28). See note on 6:1.

8:26 one thousand seven hundred shekels: About 50 pounds of earrings are collected.

8:27 ephod: Usually refers to a priestly garment made of fine linen and decorated with gold chains and shoulder pieces (Ex 28:6–14). It may be that Gideon puts forward the idea as a way of honoring the kingly rule of Yahweh (if it has sacred lots, like the high priest's vestment, these could be used to discern God's will in specific situations). Regardless, it is soon revered as an idol image (17:5). • Collecting gold earrings for the making of a cult object recalls how Aaron fashioned the golden calf at Mount Sinai from a donation of gold earrings (Ex 32:2–4). Likewise, Moses manufactured a bronze serpent for the benefit of Israel (Num 21:8–9), but it was later venerated as an idol (2 Kings 18:4). **a snare:** Despite doing the Lord's work (6:16) and defending the Lord's honor (8:23), Gideon abandons his faith in Yahweh and ends up an idolater like his father before him (6:25).

8:31 Abimelech: Means "my father is king." The name is tragically ironic, since Gideon refuses royal honor (8:23), while Abimelech seeks it with reckless abandon (9:1–6).

8:33 Baal-berith: Means "lord of the covenant", a title for the Canaanite fertility god, Baal, at Shechem. See note on 2:11.

---

*8:23: It appears from the sequel that Gideon did in fact become a king even if he refused the title; but the idea of an hereditary monarchy was still unacceptable, as the following history of Abimelech shows.

the family of Jerubba'al (that is, Gideon) in return for all the good that he had done to Israel.

Abimelech Tries to Establish a Monarchy

9 Now Abim'elech the son of Jerubba'al went to She'chem to his mother's kinsmen and said to them and to the whole clan of his mother's family, ²"Say in the ears of all the citizens of She'chem, 'Which is better for you, that all seventy of the sons of Jerubba'al rule over you, or that one rule over you?' Remember also that I am your bone and your flesh." ³And his mother's kinsmen spoke all these words on his behalf in the ears of all the men of She'chem; and their hearts inclined to follow Abim'elech, for they said, "He is our brother." ⁴And they gave him seventy pieces of silver out of the house of Ba'al-be'rith with which Abim'elech hired worthless and reckless fellows, who followed him. ⁵And he went to his father's house at Oph'rah, and slew his brothers the sons of Jerubba'al, seventy men, upon one stone; but Jo'tham the youngest son of Jerubbaal was left, for he hid himself. ⁶And all the citizens of She'chem came together, and all Beth-mil'lo, and they went and made Abim'elech king, by the oak of the pillar at Shechem.

Jotham's Parable
of the Trees, Vine, and Bramble

7 When it was told to Jo'tham, he went and stood on the top of Mount Ger'izim, and cried aloud and said to them, "Listen to me, you men of She'chem, that God may listen to you. ⁸The trees once went forth to anoint a king over them; and they said to the olive tree, 'Reign over us.' ⁹But the olive tree said to them, 'Shall I leave my fatness, by which gods and men are honored, and go to sway over the trees?' ¹⁰And the trees said to the fig tree, 'Come you, and reign over us.' ¹¹But the fig tree said to them, 'Shall I leave my sweetness and my good fruit, and go to sway over the trees?' ¹²And the trees said to the vine, 'Come you, and reign over us.' ¹³But the vine said to them, 'Shall I leave my wine which cheers gods and men, and go to sway over the trees?' ¹⁴Then all the trees said to the bramble, 'Come you, and reign over us.' ¹⁵And the bramble said to the trees, 'If in good faith you are anointing me king over you, then come and take refuge in my shade; but if not, let fire come out of the bramble and devour the cedars of Lebanon.'

16 "Now therefore, if you acted in good faith and honor when you made Abim'elech king, and if you have dealt well with Jerubba'al and his house, and have done to him as his deeds deserved—¹⁷for my father fought for you, and risked his life, and rescued you from the hand of Mid'ian; ¹⁸and you have risen up against my father's house this day, and have slain his sons, seventy men on one stone, and have made Abim'elech, the son of his maidservant, king over the citizens of She'chem, because he is your kinsman—¹⁹if you then have acted in good faith and honor with Jerubba'al and with his house this day, then rejoice in Abim'elech,

---

9:1–57 The reign of terror carried out by Gideon's son Abimelech. He is cast in the role of a ruthless anti-judge whose quest for power brings suffering to Israel rather than security. Abimelech's rule, while lasting only three years (9:22), is bloodstained by violence: he kills to attain kingship (9:5), kills to retain it (9:42–45), and is himself killed in the end (9:53–54). The point of the story is that Israel's first experiment with kingship is a total disaster, thanks to the unworthy character of Abimelech.

9:1 Jerubaal: Another name for Gideon (6:32). **Shechem:** Over 30 miles north of Jerusalem in the highlands of central Palestine. It lies within the tribal territory of Manasseh (Josh 17:1–2). Shechem is where Joshua led an earlier generation of Israelites in ratifying and renewing the Deuteronomic covenant (Josh 8:30–35; 24:1–28). Now, many years later, Shechem witnesses another generation of Israel abandoning the covenant. **his mother's kinsmen:** The relatives of Gideon's concubine from Shechem (8:31). With their assistance, Abimelech wins the backing of the city's leading citizens (9:3).

9:2 Which is better: The choice is between oligarchy (the rule of a few) and monarchy (the rule of one). **all seventy:** Born to Gideon's many wives (8:30). **your bone and your flesh:** I.e., your blood relative (Gen 29:14).

9:3 He is our brother: Abimelech is favored as a hometown candidate with family ties in Shechem. Gideon's other sons live in Ophrah (9:5).

9:4 house of Baal-berith: A local idol temple (8:33). Near Eastern sanctuaries often served as treasuries for the deposit of sacred as well as city funds. Here money is withdrawn to hire mercenary hit men. See note on 8:33.

9:5 Ophrah: See note on 6:11. **slew his brothers:** Abimelech, in order to eliminate rival claimants to his throne,

commits mass fratricide, killing 69 of his 70 half-brothers. **one stone:** Anticipates how Abimelech himself will die from the impact of a single stone (9:53).

9:6 Beth-millo: Some type of government building, perhaps the meeting and/or dwelling place of the Shechemite nobility. The Hebrew *millo'* seems to suggest an earthen platform that supports a large structure such as a fortress. **made Abimelech king:** Despite the fact that he is untested as a leader. Gideon, by contrast, was offered the crown after proving himself as a military commander (8:22). **the oak:** Possibly the landmark mentioned in 9:37.

9:7–15 Jotham's parable. It warns that nothing but disaster can come from sinister politics and power-hungry kings. Gideon and his seventy sons are represented by the noble trees that refuse royal honor, while Abimelech is the bramble shrub that accepts the crown but is fruitless and worthless.

9:7 Mount Gerizim: One of two mountains that overlook Shechem. Ironically, this was the mountain where the blessings of the Deuteronomic covenant were pronounced upon Israel (Deut 11:29), but here it resounds with "the curse of Jotham" (9:57).

9:9 gods and men: Olive oil is used in religious sacrifice (Lev 2:1, 16) and for anointing priests and kings (Lev 8:12; 1 Sam 10:1).

9:13 cheers gods: Wine is used for libation offerings (Num 15:10).

9:14 the bramble: A type of wild thorn bush, possibly the buckthorn.

9:15 the cedars of Lebanon: The proud rulers and citizens of Shechem (cf. Is 2:12–13).

9:17 my father fought for you: Jotham indicts the Shechemites for thankless disloyalty to Gideon after he delivered them from years of Midianite oppression.

and let him also rejoice in you; [20]but if not, let fire come out from Abim′elech, and devour the citizens of She′chem, and Beth-mil′lo; and let fire come out from the citizens of Shechem, and from Beth-millo, and devour Abimelech." [21]And Jo′tham ran away and fled, and went to Be′er and dwelt there, for fear of Abim′elech his brother.

The Downfall of Abimelech

22 Abim′elech ruled over Israel three years. [23]And God sent an evil spirit between Abim′elech and the men of She′chem; and the men of Shechem dealt treacherously with Abimelech; [24]that the violence done to the seventy sons of Jerubba′al might come and their blood be laid upon Abim′elech their brother, who slew them, and upon the men of She′chem, who strengthened his hands to slay his brothers. [25]And the men of She′chem put men in ambush against him on the mountain tops, and they robbed all who passed by them along that way; and it was told Abim′elech.

26 And Ga′al the son of E′bed moved into She′chem with his kinsmen; and the men of Shechem put confidence in him. [27]And they went out into the field, and gathered the grapes from their vineyards and trod them, and held festival, and went into the house of their god, and ate and drank and reviled Abim′elech. [28]And Ga′al the son of E′bed said, "Who is Abim′elech, and who are we of She′chem, that we should serve him? Did not the son of Jerubba′al and Ze′bul his officer serve the men of Ha′mor the father of Shechem? Why then should we serve him? [29]Would that this people were under my hand! then I would remove Abim′elech. I would say[1] to Abimelech, 'Increase your army, and come out.'"

30 When Ze′bul the ruler of the city heard the words of Ga′al the son of E′bed, his anger was kindled. [31]And he sent messengers to Abim′elech at Aru′mah,[m] saying, "Behold, Ga′al the son of E′bed and his kinsmen have come to She′chem, and they are stirring up[n] the city against you. [32]Now therefore, go by night, you and the men that are with you, and lie in wait in the fields. [33]Then in the morning, as soon as the sun is up, rise early and rush upon the city; and when he and the men that are with him come out against you, you may do to them as occasion offers."

34 And Abim′elech and all the men that were with him rose up by night, and laid wait against She′chem in four companies. [35]And Ga′al the son of E′bed went out and stood in the entrance of the gate of the city; and Abim′elech and the men that were with him rose from the ambush. [36]And when Ga′al saw the men, he said to Ze′bul, "Look, men are coming down from the mountain tops!" And Zebul said to him, "You see the shadow of the mountains as if they were men." [37]Ga′al spoke again and said, "Look, men are coming down from the center of the land, and one company is coming from the direction of the Diviners' Oak." [38]Then Ze′bul said to him, "Where is your mouth now, you who said, 'Who is Abim′elech, that we should serve him?' Are not these the men whom you despised? Go out now and fight with them." [39]And Ga′al went out at the head of the men of She′chem, and fought with Abim′elech. [40]And Abim′elech chased him, and he fled before him; and many fell wounded, up to the entrance of the gate. [41]And Abim′elech dwelt at Aru′mah; and Ze′bul drove out Ga′al and his kinsmen, so that they could not live on at She′chem.

42 On the following day the men went out into the fields. And Abim′elech was told. [43]He took his men and divided them into three companies, and laid wait in the fields; and he looked and saw the men coming out of the city, and he rose against them and slew them. [44]Abim′elech and the company[o] that was with him rushed forward and stood at the entrance of the gate of the city, while the two companies rushed upon all who were in the fields and slew them. [45]And Abim′elech fought against the city all that day; he took the city, and killed the people that were in it; and he razed the city and sowed it with salt.

9:21 Beer: Probably the water well mentioned in Num 21:16 that was east of the Jordan.

9:22 ruled over Israel: Abimelech governs Shechem and surrounding districts (9:18).

9:23 God sent an evil spirit: Indicates that Yahweh is sovereign over the world of spirits and that he can utilize even malevolent forces for the fulfillment of his plans. In this case, a demon is given free rein to sour the relationship between Abimelech and Shechem with distrust and contempt and thereby bring the punishment of bloodguilt upon all who were complicit in the massacre of Gideon's sons (9:56–57). God will orchestrate the downfall of King Saul in similar fashion (1 Sam 16:14). Theologically, the point is not that Yahweh is the *cause* of moral evil but that he can *make use* of evildoing for the purpose of administering divine justice.

9:25 it was told Abimelech: The presence of an informant indicates that some in Shechem are still loyal to Abimelech.

9:26 Gaal: A newcomer to Shechem who rallies the townspeople behind him. Judging from his words in 9:28, he seems to be someone whose ancestral ties with Shechem give him a credible claim to kingship. Specifically, he sells himself as a descendant of Hamor, the traditional founder of Shechem (9:28; Gen 33:19).

9:27 house of their god: Presumably the "house of Baal-berith" (9:4).

9:28 Zebul: The ruler of Shechem (9:30), while Abimelech maintains residence in nearby Arumah (9:31).

9:31 Arumah: Five miles southeast of Shechem (9:41).

9:36 You see the shadow: A clever way to buy more time by delaying Gaal's military response to the attack.

9:37 the Diviners' Oak: Otherwise unknown but possibly the same tree mentioned in 9:6.

9:45 sowed it with salt: Probably an ancient curse ritual designed to ruin farmlands and make them unproductive (cf. Deut 29:23; Zeph 2:9).

---

[1] Gk: Heb *and he said.*
[m] Cn See 9:41. Heb *Tormah.*
[n] Cn: Heb *besieging.*
[o] Vg and some Mss of Gk: Heb *companies.*

46 When all the people of the Tower of She'-chem heard of it, they entered the stronghold of the house of El-be'rith. ⁴⁷Abim'elech was told that all the people of the Tower of She'chem were gathered together. ⁴⁸And Abim'elech went up to Mount Zalmon, he and all the men that were with him; and Abimelech took an axe in his hand, and cut down a bundle of brushwood, and took it up and laid it on his shoulder. And he said to the men that were with him, "What you have seen me do, make haste to do, as I have done." ⁴⁹So every one of the people cut down his bundle and following Abim'elech put it against the stronghold, and they set the stronghold on fire over them, so that all the people of the Tower of She'chem also died, about a thousand men and women.

50 Then Abim'elech went to The'bez, and encamped against Thebez, and took it. ⁵¹But there was a strong tower within the city, and all the people of the city fled to it, all the men and women, and shut themselves in; and they went to the roof of the tower. ⁵²And Abim'elech came to the tower, and fought against it, and drew near to the door of the tower to burn it with fire. ⁵³And a certain woman threw an upper millstone upon Abim'-elech's head, and crushed his skull. ⁵⁴Then he called hastily to the young man his armor-bearer, and said to him, "Draw your sword and kill me, lest men say of me, 'A woman killed him.'" And his young man thrust him through, and he died. ⁵⁵And when the men of Israel saw that Abim'elech was dead, they departed every man to his home. ⁵⁶Thus God repaid the crime of Abim'elech, which he committed against his father in killing his seventy brothers; ⁵⁷and God also made all the wickedness of the men of She'chem fall back upon their heads, and upon them came the curse of Jo'tham the son of Jerubba'al.

Tola and Jair

10 After Abim'elech there arose to deliver Israel Tola the son of Puah, son of Dodo, a man of Is'sachar; and he lived at Sha'mir in the hill country of E'phraim. ²And he judged Israel twenty-three years. Then he died, and was buried at Sha'mir.

3 After him arose Ja'ir the Gileadite, who judged Israel twenty-two years. ⁴And he had thirty sons who rode on thirty donkeys; and they had thirty cities, called Hav'voth-ja'ir to this day, which are in the land of Gilead. ⁵And Ja'ir died, and was buried in Kamon.

Oppression by the Philistines and Ammonites

6 And the sons of Israel again did what was evil in the sight of the LORD, and served the Ba'als and the Ash'taroth, the gods of Syria, the gods of Sidon, the gods of Moab, the gods of the Am'monites, and the gods of the Philis'tines; and they forsook the LORD, and did not serve him. ⁷And the anger of the LORD was kindled against Israel, and he sold them into the hand of the Philis'tines and into the hand of the Am'monites, ⁸and they crushed and oppressed the children of Israel that year. For eighteen years they oppressed all the sons of Israel that were beyond the Jordan in the land of the Am'orites, which is in Gilead. ⁹And the Am'monites crossed the Jordan to fight also against Judah and against Benjamin and against the house of E'phraim; so that Israel was sorely distressed.

9:46 house of El-berith: The title means "house of the covenant god".

9:48 Mount Zalmon: Meaning uncertain but possibly "shadowy mountain". Some think it another name for Mount Ebal, the mountain of cursing (Deut 11:29).

9:49 set ... on fire: Fulfills the curse of Jotham (9:57) enunciated in his parable (9:15).

9:50 Thebez: Roughly ten miles north of Shechem.

9:53 upper millstone: A large circular stone that turns over the top of a lower stationary stone, grinding wheat in between. **threw:** Presumably with help from others. **crushed his skull:** The impact of the stone causes a life-threatening head injury, and yet Abimelech remains conscious for a time and fearful of being killed by a woman (9:54). His humiliating demise, remembered long afterward (2 Sam 11:21), is reminiscent of the mortal blow dealt by Jael that crushed the head of Sisera (4:21; 5:26).

9:54 kill me: Saul will make the same desperate request of his armor bearer, but without the young man's compliance (1 Sam 31:4).

10:1 Tola: A minor judge whose career is only summarized. He was both a deliverer and judge over Israel, which may mean that he reestablished law and order in the aftermath of Abimelech's tyrannical reign. **Shamir:** Otherwise unknown, though some think it an archaic name for Samaria in central Palestine.

10:3 Jair: A minor judge from Gilead, east of the Jordan. His many sons, donkeys, and cities indicate he was a man of tremendous wealth and influence. His genealogy is unmentioned, but Gilead spread across the tribal regions of Reuben, Gad, and half-Manasseh.

10:5 Kamon: Exact location unknown.

10:6—12:7 The judgeship of Jephthah, an outcast turned outlaw (11:2-3) who agrees to lead Israel against Ammonite aggressors and become the ruler of Gilead, east of the Jordan (11:4-11). Jephthah is adept at diplomacy and skilled in military leadership, and yet his career is overshadowed by family tragedy (11:29-40) and civil war between rival Israelite tribes (12:1-6). Being a descendant of Gilead (11:1), he is from the tribe of Manasseh (Josh 17:1).

10:6 the gods: Idolatry is an ever-worsening problem in Israel. The covenant people, long attached to the Canaanite deities Baal and Ashtoreth (2:13; 6:10; 8:33), have now begun to worship Syrian (Hadah), Moabite (Chemosh), Ammonite (Molech), and Philistine deities as well (Dagon) (CCC 2112-14).

10:7 Philistines: Hostile neighbors of Israel in southwest Canaan. Samson will be the judge in later chapters who weakens the power of the Philistines (13:1—16:31). See note on 3:3. **Ammonites:** Distant relatives of Israel living on the outer edge of Arabia, just east of the Transjordan tribes of Gad and Reuben (Gen 19:36-38). Jephthah will be called upon to drive Ammon out of Israel's territory (11:4-6).

10:9 Judah ... Benjamin ... Ephraim: Ammonite invaders harass not only the Transjordan tribes but even cross over into the heartland of Israel, west of the Jordan.

10 And the sons of Israel cried to the LORD, saying, "We have sinned against you, because we have forsaken our God and have served the Ba'als." ¹¹And the LORD said to the sons of Israel, "Did I not deliver you from the Egyptians and from the Am'orites, from the Am'monites and from the Philis'tines? ¹²The Sido'nians also, and the Amal'ekites, and the Ma'onites, oppressed you; and you cried to me, and I delivered you out of their hand. ¹³Yet you have forsaken me and served other gods; therefore I will deliver you no more. ¹⁴Go and cry to the gods whom you have chosen; let them deliver you in the time of your distress." ¹⁵And the sons of Israel said to the LORD, "We have sinned; do to us whatever seems good to you; only deliver us, we beg you, this day." ¹⁶So they put away the foreign gods from among them and served the LORD; and he became indignant over the misery of Israel.

17 Then the Am'monites were called to arms, and they encamped in Gilead; and the sons of Israel came together, and they encamped at Mizpah. ¹⁸And the people, the leaders of Gilead, said one to another, "Who is the man that will begin to fight against the Am'monites? He shall be head over all the inhabitants of Gilead."

Jephthah

11 Now Jephthah the Gileadite was a mighty warrior, but he was the son of a harlot. Gilead was the father of Jephthah. ²And Gilead's wife also bore him sons; and when his wife's sons grew up, they thrust Jephthah out, and said to him, "You shall not inherit in our father's house; for you are the son of another woman." ³Then Jephthah fled from his brothers, and dwelt in the land of Tob; and

worthless fellows collected round Jephthah, and went raiding with him.

4 After a time the Am'monites made war against Israel. ⁵And when the Am'monites made war against Israel, the elders of Gilead went to bring Jephthah from the land of Tob; ⁶and they said to Jephthah, "Come and be our leader, that we may fight with the Am'monites." ⁷But Jephthah said to the elders of Gilead, "Did you not hate me, and drive me out of my father's house? Why have you come to me now when you are in trouble?" ⁸And the elders of Gilead said to Jephthah, "That is why we have turned to you now, that you may go with us and fight with the Am'monites, and be our head over all the inhabitants of Gilead." ⁹Jephthah said to the elders of Gilead, "If you bring me home again to fight with the Am'monites, and the LORD gives them over to me, I will be your head." ¹⁰And the elders of Gilead said to Jephthah, "The LORD will be witness between us; we will surely do as you say." ¹¹So Jephthah went with the elders of Gilead, and the people made him head and leader over them; and Jephthah spoke all his words before the LORD at Mizpah.

12 Then Jephthah sent messengers to the king of the Am'monites and said, "What have you against me, that you have come to me to fight against my land?" ¹³And the king of the Am'monites answered the messengers of Jephthah, "Because Israel on coming from Egypt took away my land, from the Arnon to the Jabbok and to the Jordan; now therefore restore it peaceably." ¹⁴And Jephthah sent messengers again to the king of the Am'monites ¹⁵and said to him, "Thus says Jephthah: Israel did not take away the land of Moab or the land of

---

10:12 Sidonians: The people of Sidon, a coastal city northwest of Israel (3:3). **Amalekites:** A nomadic people from the Sinai Peninsula, hostile to Israel since the time of the Exodus (Ex 17:8–16). **Maonites:** Identity unknown. The Greek LXX has "Midianites", referring back to the opponents defeated by Gideon (8:28; 9:17).

10:13 I will deliver you no more: A rebuke against Israel for its repeated acts of apostasy and idolatry. Formally, the statement sounds like a divine renunciation of the covenant, but, functionally, it aims to elicit a deeper level of repentance from the people.

10:14 cry to the gods: A summons to recognize the futility of idol worship (Jer 2:28).

10:16 put away the foreign gods: A renunciation of pagan idols and a renewal of Israel's commitment to the Lord (Josh 24:14). **he became indignant:** It is disputed whether this statement expresses **(1)** divine annoyance with Israel's infidelity or **(2)** divine compassion for Israel's distress. The former seems more likely in view of the preceding verses.

10:17 Mizpah: A settlement in Gilead, east of the Jordan (11:29). Another town of the same name lies within the territory of Benjamin (1 Sam 7:5).

11:1 son of a harlot: Explains why Jephthah is treated like an illegitimate son and driven from his father's house by his half-brothers (11:2).

11:3 the land of Tob: On the eastern outskirts of Gilead. **worthless fellows:** Recalls the mercenary thugs hired by Abimelech (9:4).

11:4 Ammonites: Eastern neighbors of Israel. See note on 10:7.

11:6 Come and be our leader: Recalls the offer to make Gideon ruler of Israel in 8:22, only here civic leadership is restricted to Israelites dwelling east of the Jordan.

11:10 witness between us: An oath formula that invokes Yahweh to oversee and enforce the terms of the covenant agreement.

11:11 before the LORD: Suggests the installation ceremony is solemnized by some type of oath of office. **Mizpah:** East of the Jordan. See note on 10:17.

11:13 the Arnon: A river flowing into the middle of the Dead Sea from the east. It formed the northern border of Moab at the time of the Israelite conquest (11:18). Israel camps north of the Arnon on the so-called plains of Moab before entering the land (Num 22:1). **the Jabbok:** A river flowing into the lower course of the Jordan from the east.

11:15-27 Jephthah's diplomatic address to the Ammonites. He contests the claim that Israel illegally occupies lands east of the Jordan since **(1)** Israel seized this territory from the Amorites, not the Ammonites (11:21-22); **(2)** the Lord gave it to Israel as a possession (11:23); and **(3)** Israel has occupied this region for 300 years without Ammon objecting or pressing claims of rightful ownership (11:26). For the biblical background summarized by Jephthah, see Num 21:10-35 and Deut 2:1-3:22.

the Am'monites, [16]but when they came up from Egypt, Israel went through the wilderness to the Red Sea and came to Ka'desh. [17]Israel then sent messengers to the king of E'dom, saying, 'Let us pass, we beg, through your land'; but the king of Edom would not listen. And they sent also to the king of Moab, but he would not consent. So Israel remained at Ka'desh. [18]Then they journeyed through the wilderness, and went around the land of E'dom and the land of Moab, and arrived on the east side of the land of Moab, and camped on the other side of the Arnon; but they did not enter the territory of Moab, for the Arnon was the boundary of Moab. [19]Israel then sent messengers to Si'hon king of the Am'orites, king of Heshbon; and Israel said to him, 'Let us pass, we beg, through your land to our country.' [20]But Si'hon did not trust Israel to pass through his territory; so Sihon gathered all his people together, and encamped at Ja'haz, and fought with Israel. [21]And the LORD, the God of Israel, gave Si'hon and all his people into the hand of Israel, and they defeated them; so Israel took possession of all the land of the Am'orites, who inhabited that country. [22]And they took possession of all the territory of the Am'orites from the Arnon to the Jabbok and from the wilderness to the Jordan. [23]So then the LORD, the God of Israel, dispossessed the Am'orites from before his people Israel; and are you to take possession of them? [24]Will you not possess what Che'mosh your god gives you to possess? And all that the LORD our God has dispossessed before us, we will possess. [25]Now are you any better than Balak the son of Zippor, king of Moab? Did he ever strive against Israel, or did he ever go to war with them? [26]While Israel dwelt in Heshbon and its villages, and in Aro'er and its villages, and in all the cities that are on the banks of the Arnon, three hundred years, why did you not recover them within that time? [27]I therefore have not sinned against you, and you do me wrong by making war on me; the LORD, the Judge, decide this day between the sons of Israel and the people of Ammon." [28]But the king of the Am'monites did not heed the message of Jephthah which he sent to him.

Jephthah's Vow

29 Then the Spirit of the LORD came upon Jephthah, and he passed through Gilead and Manas'seh, and passed on to Mizpah of Gilead, and from Mizpah of Gilead he passed on to the Am'monites. [30]And Jephthah made a vow to the LORD, and said, "If you will give the Am'monites into my hand, [31]then whoever comes forth from the doors of my house to meet me, when I return victorious from the Am'monites, shall be the LORD's, and I will offer him up for a burnt offering." [32]So Jephthah crossed over to the Am'monites to fight against them; and the LORD gave them into his hand. [33]And he struck them from Aro'er to the neighborhood of Minnith, twenty cities, and as far as A'bel-ker'amim, with a very great slaughter. So the Am'monites were subdued before the sons of Israel.

11:24 Chemosh: National god of the Moabites (Num 21:29). It may be that Jephthah makes reference to Chemosh (instead of the Ammonite national god, Molech) because Ammon at this point appears to be in possession of former Moabite lands, south of the Arnon. In any case, according to the Torah, Yahweh gave the Ammonites their land (Deut 2:19).

11:25 Balak: The Moabite king who conspired to curse Israel in the wilderness (Num 22:1–6).

11:26 three hundred years: The length of time Israel has been settled in lands east of the Jordan. This historical notation coheres with the chronology of 1 Kings 6:1, which puts the Exodus from Egypt 480 years before Solomon's fourth year as king. On this calculation, Israel's seizure of the Transjordan took place before 1400 B.C.

11:27 the Lord, the Judge: A reminder that the human judges of the book, major and minor, are merely agents of Yahweh's justice. • Jephthah's confidence that God is Lord of all lands and that he will judge matters in Israel's favor is the faith celebrated in Heb 11:32–34.

11:29–40 Jephthah's vow and its fulfillment. Inadvertently but recklessly, he promises to sacrifice his unmarried daughter, an only child, as an offering to the Lord. The predicament is of his own making and means that Jephthah's daughter is destined to die childless and his family line is doomed to extinction. There is some debate about the nature of the sacrifice involved. **(1)** A majority of commentators, ancient and modern, hold that Jephthah speaks literally of a "burnt offering" (11:31) and that he carries out his vow by slaying his daughter as a human sacrifice (cf. 2 Kings 3:27; Jer 19:5), despite the stern condemnation of this practice in the Torah (Lev 20:1–5;

Deut 12:31; 18:10). On this reading, Jephthah shows himself to be a man of his evil times—morally debased and misguided in his actions on top of being foolish and thoughtless in his words. **(2)** A few commentators hold that Jephthah speaks metaphorically about a "burnt offering" and that he pledges to dedicate his daughter to Yahweh (cf. 1 Sam 1:11), perhaps as one of the ministering women who serve at Israel's sanctuary (Ex 38:8; 1 Sam 2:22). Although evidence for such a custom is much later, it may be that females who served in this capacity were virgins (e.g., *Protevangelium of James* 7–10). On this reading, Jephthah's actions are commendable rather than cruel; it could also help to explain why his daughter mourns her virginity rather than her imminent demise (11:37–38). See note on 1 Sam 2:22.

11:29 the Spirit: The empowering presence of God. See note on 3:10.

11:30 a vow: A conditional promise made to God and often expressed in the form of an "if ... then ..." statement (cf. Gen 28:20–22; Num 21:2). Taking a vow is voluntary, but once such a pledge is made, one is normally obligated to fulfill it (Num 30:3). • Some actions are good in themselves and, thus, suitable matters for a vow, yet they may yield an evil result, in which case the vow should not be fulfilled. This is the situation with Jephthah's vow, where an evil result is in fact possible, were he to meet an animal unfit for sacrifice or, as it turned out, a human being (St. Thomas Aquinas, *Summa Theologiae* II-II, 88, 2).

11:31 burnt offering: A holocaust sacrifice in which the entire victim is burned upon the altar and rises to heaven as smoke (Lev 1:3–9).

11:33 Minnith ... Abel-keramim: Locations unknown.

Jephthah's Daughter

34 Then Jephthah came to his home at Mizpah;
and behold, his daughter came out to meet him with
timbrels and with dances; she was his only child;
beside her he had neither son nor daughter. 35And
when he saw her, he tore his clothes, and said, "Alas,
my daughter! you have brought me very low, and
you have become the cause of great trouble to me; for
I have opened my mouth to the LORD, and I cannot
take back my vow." 36And she said to him, "My father,
if you have opened your mouth to the LORD, do to me
according to what has gone forth from your mouth,
now that the LORD has avenged you on your enemies,
on the Am′monites." 37And she said to her father, "Let
this thing be done for me; let me alone two months,
that I may go and wander[p] on the mountains, and
bewail my virginity, I and my companions." 38And he
said, "Go." And he sent her away for two months; and
she departed, she and her companions, and bewailed
her virginity upon the mountains. 39And at the end of
two months, she returned to her father, who did with
her according to his vow which he had made.* She
had never known a man. And it became a custom in
Israel 40that the daughters of Israel went year by year
to lament the daughter of Jephthah the Gileadite four
days in the year.

Intertribal Fighting

12 The men of E′phraim were called to arms,
and they crossed to Za′phon and said to
Jephthah, "Why did you cross over to fight against
the Am′monites, and did not call us to go with
you? We will burn your house over you with fire."
2And Jephthah said to them, "I and my people had a
great feud with the Am′monites; and when I called
you, you did not deliver me from their hand. 3And
when I saw that you would not deliver me, I took
my life in my hand, and crossed over against the
Am′monites, and the LORD gave them into my hand;
why then have you come up to me this day, to fight
against me?" 4Then Jephthah gathered all the men
of Gilead and fought with E′phraim; and the men of
Gilead struck Ephraim, because they said, "You are
fugitives of Ephraim, you Gileadites, in the midst of
Ephraim and Manas′seh." 5And the Gileadites took
the fords of the Jordan against the E′phraimites. And
when any of the fugitives of E′phraim said, "Let me
go over," the men of Gilead said to him, "Are you an
Ephraimite?" When he said, "No," 6they said to him,
"Then say Shib′boleth," and he said, "Sib′boleth," for
he could not pronounce it right; then they seized him
and slew him at the fords of the Jordan. And there fell
at that time forty-two thousand of the E′phraimites.
7 Jephthah judged Israel six years. Then Jephthah the Gileadite died, and was buried in his city
in Gilead.[q]

Ibzan, Elon, and Abdon

8 After him Ibzan of Bethlehem judged Israel.
9He had thirty sons; and thirty daughters he gave
in marriage outside his clan, and thirty daughters
he brought in from outside for his sons. And he
judged Israel seven years. 10Then Ibzan died, and
was buried at Bethlehem.
11 After him E′lon the Zeb′ulunite judged Israel;
and he judged Israel ten years. 12Then E′lon the
Zeb′ulunite died, and was buried at Ai′jalon in
the land of Zeb′ulun.
13 After him Abdon the son of Hillel the Pir′a-
thonite judged Israel. 14He had forty sons and thirty

11:34 timbrels ... dances: Victory celebrations were traditionally led by the women in ancient Israel (Ex 15:20; 1 Sam 18:6). **only child:** The same expression (Heb., *yaḥid*) is used to describe Isaac when Abraham is asked to sacrifice him as a burnt offering (Gen 22:2). The two events are mirror opposites: In Genesis 22, God commands the sacrifice of Isaac but intervenes to stop Abraham from carrying it out; in Judges 11, God neither commands Jephthah to sacrifice his daughter nor intervenes to prevent it from taking place (cf. St. Augustine, *Questions on Judges* 49, 4).

11:35 tore his clothes: A sign of extreme distress (Gen 37:34).

11:37 virginity: Lamented because Jephthah's daughter will never marry and become a mother (11:39). This is a painful burden (Gen 30:1) since children are viewed as signs of God's blessing (Gen 1:28; Ps 128:3–4). Only gradually is sexual abstinence esteemed to be something conducive to spiritual growth and undistracted ministry (Ex 19:15; Mt 19:12; 1 Cor 7:7–8, 38) (CCC 2349).

11:39 a custom: A festival of mournful remembrance, otherwise unmentioned in the OT.

[p] Cn: Heb *go down*.
[q] Gk: Heb *in the cities of Gilead*.
* 11:39: Human sacrifice, common in Canaan and surrounding lands, was never permitted in Israel; cf. Lev 18:21. The few cases we find were due to foreign influence or to an erroneous conscience; cf. 2 Sam 21:4–6; 2 Kings 23:10.

12:1–6 Intertribal tensions explode into intertribal warfare. The clash is between the tribe of Ephraim, settled in central Canaan, and the tribes of Gilead (Reuben, Gad, half-Manasseh) settled east of the Jordan. The Ephraimites are offended that Jephthah never called on them to join the war effort against Ammon, and so they pledge retribution (12:1). Jephthah, for his part, claims to have issued a summons that went unheeded (12:2–3), although there is no mention of this in the preceding narrative. It seems that Ephraim, one of the largest and strongest of the twelve tribes, is challenging Jephthah's leadership in Israel.

12:1 Zaphon: A town just east of the Jordan in Gilead (Josh 13:25–27).

12:4 You are fugitives: A taunting insult.

12:6 Shibboleth: Means "ear of grain" or "flood of waters". **could not pronounce it right:** Fleeing Ephraimites are exposed at a Jordan River checkpoint by pronouncing the first consonant of Shibboleth as "s" whereas the tribes in Gilead pronounced it "sh". **forty-two thousand:** A horrific massacre of fellow Israelites, exceeding all other casualty figures in the book.

12:7 his city: Mizpah (11:34).

12:8 Ibzan: A minor judge and father of 60 children, by whom he made marriage alliances with other clans. **Bethlehem:** Probably not the town of this name in Judah but the town of Bethlehem belonging to Zebulun (Josh 19:15).

12:11 Elon: A minor judge from the tribe of Zebulun in lower Galilee.

12:13 Abdon: A minor judge from the tribe of Ephraim. His hometown and burial place is Pirathon, a village southwest

grandsons, who rode on seventy donkeys; and he judged Israel eight years. ¹⁵Then Abdon the son of Hillel the Pir′athonite died, and was buried at Pir′athon in the land of E′phraim, in the hill country of the Amal′ekites.

The Birth of Samson

13 * And the sons of Israel again did what was evil in the sight of the LORD; and the LORD gave them into the hand of the Philis′tines for forty years.

2 And there was a certain man of Zorah, of the tribe of the Da′nites, whose name was Mano′ah; and his wife was barren and had no children. ³And the angel of the LORD appeared to the woman and said to her, "Behold, you are barren and have no children; but you shall conceive and bear a son. ⁴Therefore beware, and drink no wine or strong drink, and eat nothing unclean, ⁵for behold, you shall conceive and bear a son. No razor shall come upon his head, for the boy shall be a Naz′irite to God from birth; and he shall begin to deliver Israel from the hand of the Philis′tines." ⁶Then the woman came and told her husband, "A man of God came to me, and his countenance was like the countenance of the angel of God, very terrible; I did not ask him where he was from, and he did not tell me his name; ⁷but he said to me, 'Behold, you shall conceive and bear a son; so then drink no wine or strong drink, and eat nothing unclean, for the boy shall be a Naz′irite to God from birth to the day of his death.'"

8 Then Mano′ah entreated the LORD, and said, "O, LORD, I beg you, let the man of God whom you sent come again to us, and teach us what we are to do with the boy that will be born." ⁹And God listened to the voice of Mano′ah, and the angel of God came again to the woman as she sat in the field; but Manoah her husband was not with her. ¹⁰And the woman ran in haste and told her husband, "Behold, the man who came to me the other day has appeared to me." ¹¹And Mano′ah arose and went after his wife, and came to the man and said to him, "Are you the man who spoke to this woman?" And he said, "I am." ¹²And Mano′ah said, "Now when your words come true, what is to be the boy's manner of life, and what is he to do?" ¹³And the angel of the LORD said to Mano′ah, "Of all that I said to the woman let her beware. ¹⁴She may not eat of anything that comes from the vine, neither let her drink wine or strong drink, or eat any unclean thing; all that I commanded her let her observe."

15 Mano′ah said to the angel of the LORD, "Please, let us detain you, and prepare a kid for you." ¹⁶And the angel of the LORD said to Mano′ah, "If you detain me, I will not eat of your food; but if you make ready a burnt offering, then offer it to the LORD." (For Manoah did not know that he was the angel of the LORD.) ¹⁷And Mano′ah said to the angel of the LORD, "What is your name, so that, when your words come true, we may honor you?" ¹⁸And the angel of the LORD said to him, "Why do you ask my name, seeing

---

13:4, 5: Lk 1:15.

---

of Shechem, and he seems to have been a man of wealth and influence.

13:1—16:31 The judgeship of Samson, the Danite strongman, whose bravery and brawn single-handedly weaken the power of the Philistines over Israel. He is the last of the judges mentioned in the book, and, even more than his predecessors, he is impelled by the "Spirit of the LORD" to accomplish his mission (13:25; 14:6, 19; 15:14). Still, Samson is a tragic figure who is ruled by his passions (14:2, 19; 16:1), who is handed over to the enemy by his own people (15:11–13), and whose personal fascination with foreign women (14:2; 16:1, 4) epitomizes Israel's national fascination with foreign gods (2:17; 10:6). Despite his many failings, Samson renews his faith in the end and dies a hero in a life-giving act of sacrifice (16:28–30). Of the many lessons conveyed by his story, one is that God can fulfill his purposes in spite of the faults of the people he uses to achieve them.

13:1 Philistines: In control of southwest Canaan. See note on 3:3.

13:2 Zorah: Nearly 18 miles west of Jerusalem, near the edge of Philistine territory. It lay in the tribal territory of Dan (Josh 19:41). **Manoah:** His name means "rest". **barren:** As were the wives of the patriarchs, Sarah, Rebekah, and Rachel (Gen 11:30; 25:21; 29:31), before God intervened and blessed them with children (Gen 21:1-2; 25:21; 30:22-23).

13:3 angel of the LORD: A heavenly messenger who speaks and acts in Yahweh's name yet assumes the appearance of a man (13:6). See word study: *Angel of the LORD* at Gen 16:7. **you shall ... bear a son:** Several birth announcements are delivered by an angel or prophet in Scripture (Gen 18:10; Is 7:14; Lk 1:13, 31; CCC 332).

13:4 eat nothing unclean: Abstaining from proscribed foods was one of the requirements for maintaining personal holiness in Israel (Lev 11:1-47).

13:5 Nazirite: One who is set apart and consecrated to God in a special way. Nazirites vowed to abstain from drinking wine and eating grapes, from cutting their hair, and from making physical contact with death (Num 6:1-8). Normally the vow was taken voluntarily and its obligations were temporary. Samson is unusual for being consecrated as a lifelong Nazirite before his birth (13:7), and yet he will show himself less than committed to living within its limits, e.g., when he hosts a drinking feast (14:10), when his hair is shorn (16:19), when he touches an animal carcass (14:8–9), and when he storms off to slay the enemy in mass numbers (14:19; 15:8, 15). • Samson prefigures John the Baptist, whose mother is initially barren (Lk 1:7), whose birth is announced by an angel (Lk 1:13), and whose designation as a Nazirite is made before his birth (Lk 1:15). **begin to deliver:** Hints that Samson will score several victories against the Philistines, but they will remain a threat to Israel after his death.

13:12 when your words come true: An expression of Manoah's faith (also in 13:17).

13:15 prepare a kid: Preparation of a young goat recalls Gideon's hospitality (6:19).

13:18 it is wonderful: I.e., incomprehensible to human minds (Ps 139:6).

---

*13:1: The "Samson cycle" (chapters 13–16) is built on the theme of the broken vow; cf. 13:4–5. This gives a religious character to what otherwise has the appearance of profane literature.

it is wonderful?" ¹⁹So Mano'ah took the kid with the cereal offering, and offered it upon the rock to the LORD, to him who works ʳ wonders. ˢ ²⁰And when the flame went up toward heaven from the altar, the angel of the LORD ascended in the flame of the altar while Mano'ah and his wife looked on; and they fell on their faces to the ground.

21 The angel of the LORD appeared no more to Mano'ah and to his wife. Then Manoah knew that he was the angel of the LORD. ²²And Mano'ah said to his wife, "We shall surely die, for we have seen God." ²³But his wife said to him, "If the LORD had meant to kill us, he would not have accepted a burnt offering and a cereal offering at our hands, or shown us all these things, or now announced to us such things as these." ²⁴And the woman bore a son, and called his name Samson; and the boy grew, and the LORD blessed him. ²⁵And the Spirit of the LORD began to stir him in Ma'haneh-dan, between Zorah and Esh'ta-ol.

Samson's Marriage at Timnah

14 Samson went down to Timnah, and at Timnah he saw one of the daughters of the Philis'tines. ²Then he came up, and told his father and mother, "I saw one of the daughters of the Philis'tines at Timnah; now get her for me as my wife." ³But his father and mother said to him, "Is there not a woman among the daughters of your kinsmen, or among all our people, that you must go to take a wife from the uncircumcised Philis'tines?"

But Samson said to his father, "Get her for me; for she pleases me well."

4 His father and mother did not know that it was from the LORD; for he was seeking an occasion against the Philis'tines. At that time the Philistines had dominion over Israel.

5 Then Samson went down with his father and mother to Timnah, and he came to the vineyards of Timnah. And behold, a young lion roared against him; ⁶and the Spirit of the LORD came mightily upon him, and he tore the lion asunder as one tears a kid; and he had nothing in his hand. But he did not tell his father or his mother what he had done. ⁷Then he went down and talked with the woman; and she pleased Samson well. ⁸And after a while he returned to take her; and he turned aside to see the carcass of the lion, and behold, there was a swarm of bees in the body of the lion, and honey. ⁹He scraped it out into his hands, and went on, eating as he went; and he came to his father and mother, and gave some to them, and they ate. But he did not tell them that he had taken the honey from the carcass of the lion.

10 And his father went down to the woman, and Samson made a feast there; for so the young men used to do. ¹¹And when the people saw him, they brought thirty companions to be with him. ¹²And Samson said to them, "Let me now put a riddle to you; if you can tell me what it is, within the seven

---

13:24: Lk 2:40.

13:19 the rock: Serves as a natural altar, rough and untooled (Ex 20:25).
13:20 ascended in the flame: Implies that the angel carries the sacrifice to heaven. It is also a sign that the Lord has accepted the burnt offering (13:23). For similar signs of divine acceptance, see 6:21 and Lev 9:24.
13:22 surely die: Gazing upon God with human eyes is feared as something potentially deadly (6:22; Gen 16:13; 32:30).
13:24 Samson: His name is related to the Hebrew word for "sun" (*shemesh*). The importance of this will be revealed later, when his power is eclipsed by the trickery of Delilah, whose name resembles the Hebrew word for "night" (*laylah*).
13:25 Mahaneh-dan: Means "camp of Dan", perhaps a military outpost in the territory assigned to Dan, directly west of Benjamin stretching toward the Mediterranean coast (Josh 19:40-48). For the origin of the place name, see 18:11-12.
14:1 Timnah: Less than five miles west of Samson's hometown of Zorah (13:2).
14:3 Is there not a woman ...?: Samson's parents have strong reservations about a mixed marriage. The Mosaic Law forbids Israelites to intermarry with the pagan peoples of Canaan (Deut 7:1-4). The danger is that Israel will be led astray from the Lord, as evidenced in 3:5-6 (CCC 1634). **your kinsmen:** Marriage between couples of the same tribe was encouraged in Israel (Num 36:5-9). **uncircumcised:** A derogatory epithet for Philistines (15:18), who, unlike several Semitic peoples of the Near East (Jer 9:25-26), do not practice male

circumcision (1 Sam 14:6; 17:26; 1 Chron 10:4). **she pleases me well:** Literally, "she is right in my eyes." Anticipating the appearance of this idiom in 17:6 and 21:25, the author hints that Samson typifies the waywardness of Israel as a whole during the time of the judges.
14:4 from the LORD: God will use Samson's attraction to the Philistine woman as a means to bring judgment on her people. The text says nothing to indicate that Yahweh incites or even approves of his sexual desire for her.
14:5 young lion: Once a common predator in Canaan (1 Sam 17:34).
14:6 the Spirit: The empowering presence of God. See note on 3:10.
14:9 honey from the carcass: The food is rendered unclean by its contact with the dead lion, which Levitical law designates an unclean animal (Lev 11:27). Touching the carcass is also a transgression of Samson's consecration as a Nazirite (Num 6:6). Hence, Samson does not reveal the source of the honey to his parents. • *Allegorically*, the Lord is the lion of the tribe of Judah who was slain, and from his body, the Church, comes the honey of wise teaching for his people (St. Ambrose, *The Holy Spirit* 2, 9).
14:10 a feast: The Hebrew *mishteh* more specifically means "drinking feast", which implies that Samson violates the Nazirite prohibition against drinking wine (13:4; Num 6:1-3). The event is a weeklong wedding celebration (14:12; cf. Tob 11:19).
14:11 thirty companions: Assistants for the marriage banquet.
14:12 linen ... festal garments: Undergarments and outer garments, respectively.

ʳ Gk Vg: Heb *and working*.
ˢ Heb *wonders, while Manoah and his wife looked on.*

days of the feast, and find it out, then I will give you thirty linen garments and thirty festal garments; [13]but if you cannot tell me what it is, then you shall give me thirty linen garments and thirty festal garments." And they said to him, "Put your riddle, that we may hear it." [14]And he said to them,

"Out of the eater came something to eat.

Out of the strong came something sweet."

And they could not in three days tell what the riddle was.

15 On the fourth[t] day they said to Samson's wife, "Entice your husband to tell us what the riddle is, lest we burn you and your father's house with fire. Have you invited us here to impoverish us?" [16]And Samson's wife wept before him, and said, "You only hate me, you do not love me; you have put a riddle to my countrymen, and you have not told me what it is." And he said to her, "Behold, I have not told my father nor my mother, and shall I tell you?" [17]She wept before him the seven days that their feast lasted; and on the seventh day he told her, because she pressed him hard. Then she told the riddle to her countrymen. [18]And the men of the city said to him on the seventh day before the sun went down,

"What is sweeter than honey?

What is stronger than a lion?"

And he said to them,

"If you had not plowed with my heifer,

you would not have found out my riddle."

[19]And the Spirit of the LORD came mightily upon him, and he went down to Ash'kelon and killed thirty men of the town, and took their spoil and gave the festal garments to those who had told the riddle. In hot anger he went back to his father's house. [20]And Samson's wife was given to his companion, who had been his best man.

Samson Defeats the Philistines

15 After a while, at the time of wheat harest, Samson went to visit his wife with a kid; and he said, "I will go in to my wife in the chamber." But her father would not allow him to go in. [2]And her father said, "I really thought that you utterly hated her; so I gave her to your companion. Is not her younger sister fairer than she? Please take her instead." [3]And Samson said to them, "This time I shall be blameless in regard to the Philis'tines, when I do them mischief." [4]So Samson went and caught three hundred foxes, and took torches; and he turned them tail to tail, and put a torch between each pair of tails. [5]And when he had set fire to the torches, he let the foxes go into the standing grain of the Philis'tines, and burned up the shocks and the standing grain, as well as the olive orchards. [6]Then the Philis'tines said, "Who has done this?" And they said, "Samson, the son-in-law of the Timnite, because he has taken his wife and given her to his companion." And the Philistines came up, and burned her and her father with fire. [7]And Samson said to them, "If this is what you do, I swear I will be avenged upon you, and after that I will quit." [8]And he struck them hip and thigh with great slaughter; and he went down and stayed in the cleft of the rock of E'tam.

9 Then the Philis'tines came up and encamped in Judah, and made a raid on Lehi. [10]And the men of Judah said, "Why have you come up against us?" They said, "We have come up to bind Samson, to do to him as he did to us." [11]Then three thousand men of Judah went down to the cleft of the rock of E'tam, and said to Samson, "Do you not know that the Philis'tines are rulers over us? What then is this that you have done to us?" And he said to them, "As they did to me, so have I done to them." [12]And they said to him, "We have come down to bind you, that we

---

14:15 burn ... with fire: Similar to the Ephraimite threat in 12:1.

14:17 he told her: Anticipates how Samson will yield to the prodding of Delilah in 16:16–17. Both stories have the same basic plotline: Samson sees and desires a Philistine woman who presses to learn his secret and who betrays him to her people, leading to his downfall.

14:18 my heifer: Samson's new bride.

14:19 Ashkelon: One of the five Philistine cities in southwest Canaan. See note on 3:3.

14:20 best man: Samson's personal wedding attendant among the 30 mentioned in 14:11. In later Judaism, this individual was known as "the friend" of the bridegroom (Jn 3:29).

15:1 wheat harvest: In late spring. **visit his wife:** Samson's bride continues to live with her family after the wedding, though the reasons for this are unclear. **a kid:** A young goat brought as a gift (as in 6:19). **I will go in:** With the intent to have marital relations.

15:2 hated her: Samson's father-in-law thinks his newly married daughter is despised and abandoned—hence, in need of a new husband. It is also possible that the verb "hate" refers to divorce. It is elsewhere connected with divorce (translated

"dislikes" in Deut 24:3), and in later times it functions as a semi-technical term in Jewish divorce certificates (e.g., *Elephantine papyri*). **take her instead:** A quick attempt at fixing a terrible mistake.

15:3 mischief: The coming retribution for robbing Samson of his lawful wife.

15:4 foxes: The Hebrew term can also mean "jackals" (as in Lam 5:18).

15:5 shocks: Wheat stalks already cut and bound.

15:6 burned her: Threatened in 14:15 but carried out for a different reason, namely, for her involvement with Samson, who decimated local Philistine food supplies.

15:8 struck them hip and thigh: Apparently an idiom for "a crippling victory". **the rock of Etam:** Location uncertain but possibly in the territory of Simeon (1 Chron 4:32) between Bethlehem and Tekoa (2 Chron 11:6).

15:9 encamped in Judah: Samson has pushed the Philistines to the brink of war with Israel, putting his own people in danger. **Lehi:** On the western edge of the hill country of Judah, near Philistine lands. It is an abbreviation for Ramath-lehi, which translates "Hill of the Jawbone" (15:17).

15:11 three thousand men: A force large enough to capture and extradite Samson. The Judahites' willingness to surrender him is an attempt to avoid a broader war with the Philistines.

---

[t] Gk Syr: Heb *seventh.*

may give you into the hands of the Philis'tines." And Samson said to them, "Swear to me that you will not fall upon me yourselves." ¹³They said to him, "No; we will only bind you and give you into their hands; we will not kill you." So they bound him with two new ropes, and brought him up from the rock.

14 When he came to Lehi, the Philis'tines came shouting to meet him; and the Spirit of the Lord came mightily upon him, and the ropes which were on his arms became as flax that has caught fire, and his bonds melted off his hands. ¹⁵And he found a fresh jawbone of a donkey, and put out his hand and seized it, and with it he slew a thousand men. ¹⁶And Samson said,

"With the jawbone of a donkey,
     heaps upon heaps,
with the jawbone of a donkey
     have I slain a thousand men."

¹⁷When he had finished speaking, he threw away the jawbone out of his hand; and that place was called Ra'math-le'hi.ᵘ

18 And he was very thirsty, and he called on the Lord and said, "You have granted this great deliverance by the hand of your servant; and shall I now die of thirst, and fall into the hands of the uncircumcised?" ¹⁹And God split open the hollow place that is at Lehi, and there came water from it; and when he drank, his spirit returned, and he revived. Therefore the name of it was called En-hakkor'e;ᵛ it is at Lehi to this day. ²⁰And he judged Israel in the days of the Philis'tines twenty years.

Samson and Delilah

16 Samson went to Gaza, and there he saw a harlot, and he went in to her. ²The Gazites

were told, "Samson has come here," and they surrounded the place and lay in wait for him all night at the gate of the city. They kept quiet all night, saying, "Let us wait till the light of the morning; then we will kill him." ³But Samson lay till midnight, and at midnight he arose and took hold of the doors of the gate of the city and the two posts, and pulled them up, bar and all, and put them on his shoulders and carried them to the top of the hill that is before He'bron.

4 After this he loved a woman in the valley of Sorek, whose name was Deli'lah. ⁵And the lords of the Philis'tines came to her and said to her, "Entice him, and see wherein his great strength lies, and by what means we may overpower him, that we may bind him to subdue him; and we will each give you eleven hundred pieces of silver." ⁶And Deli'lah said to Samson, "Please tell me wherein your great strength lies, and how you might be bound, that one could subdue you." ⁷And Samson said to her, "If they bind me with seven fresh bowstrings which have not been dried, then I shall become weak, and be like any other man." ⁸Then the lords of the Philis'tines brought her seven fresh bowstrings which had not been dried, and she bound him with them. ⁹Now she had men lying in wait in an inner chamber. And she said to him, "The Philis'tines are upon you, Samson!" But he snapped the bowstrings, as a tow line snaps when it touches the fire. So the secret of his strength was not known.

10 And Deli'lah said to Samson, "Behold, you have mocked me, and told me lies; please tell me how you might be bound." ¹¹And he said to her, "If they bind me with new ropes that have not been

---

15:13 two new ropes: These will prove insufficient, since nothing short of bronze shackles could restrain the mighty Samson (16:21).

15:14 the Spirit: The empowering presence of God. See note on 3:10.

15:15 fresh: Stiff and strong rather than old and brittle. **jawbone of a donkey:** A make-shift weapon reminiscent of Shamgar's oxgoad, which also inflicted mass casualties on the Philistines (3:31).

15:18 called on the Lord: One of two times in Judges that Samson is moved to prayer (the other is 16:28). Both times God responds to his plea with a miracle (15:19; 16:30). **this great deliverance:** A partial fulfillment of the angel's words in 13:5.

15:19 the hollow place: A cave or geological depression of some sort. **water:** Brings to mind the water that gushed from the wilderness rock and refreshed the parched Exodus pilgrims (Ex 17:6; Num 20:11).

15:20 twenty years: The length of Samson's judgeship, also noted in 16:31. The Philistine oppression of Israel lasted twice as long (13:1).

16:1–31 The story of Samson concludes with two parallel episodes (16:1–3 and 16:4–31). Both shine a light on his weakness for women, his superhuman strength, and the plotting of his enemies against him.

16:1 Gaza: One of the five Philistine cities in southwest Canaan. See note on 3:3. **went in to her:** A euphemism for sexual relations in a private setting (Gen 16:4).

16:3 pulled them up ... carried them: Another miraculous feat, showing Samson to be unstoppable from a human point of view. • Some read this episode as an allusion to God's promise made to Abraham that his "descendants shall possess the gate of their enemies" (Gen 22:17). **Hebron:** In southern Judah, an uphill climb of nearly 40 miles from Gaza.

16:4–22 The story of Samson and Delilah, which revolves around the "secret" of Samson's strength (16:9). Delilah is the first woman he is said to have loved (16:4), yet the Philistine temptress betrays him for money (16:5), hounds him for information (16:16), and shows contempt for his undoing (16:19). Blinded by love at first, Samson is blinded by his enemies in the end (16:21).

16:4 valley of Sorek: Stretches from the coastal plain into the highlands west of Jerusalem. **Delilah:** For the significance of her name, see note on 13:24.

16:5 lords of the Philistines: Government officials, perhaps leaders of the five major cities of Philistia. See note on 3:3. **eleven hundred pieces:** A huge amount of silver, although its modern equivalency is uncertain.

16:7 fresh bowstrings: Teasing rather than truthful words. Samson's admission that his strength could be lost is unintentionally prophetic (16:19).

16:11 new ropes: Have already proven to be an ineffective restraint in 15:13–14.

ᵘ That is *The hill of the jawbone.*
ᵛ That is *The spring of him who called.*

used, then I shall become weak, and be like any other man." ¹²So Deli′lah took new ropes and bound him with them, and said to him, "The Philis′tines are upon you, Samson!" And the men lying in wait were in an inner chamber. But he snapped the ropes off his arms like a thread.

13 And Deli′lah said to Samson, "Until now you have mocked me, and told me lies; tell me how you might be bound." And he said to her, "If you weave the seven locks of my head with the web and make it tight with the pin, then I shall become weak, and be like any other man." ¹⁴So while he slept, Deli′lah took the seven locks of his head and wove them into the web.ʷ And she made them tight with the pin, and said to him, "The Philis′tines are upon you, Samson!" But he awoke from his sleep, and pulled away the pin, the loom, and the web.

15 And she said to him, "How can you say, 'I love you,' when your heart is not with me? You have mocked me these three times, and you have not told me wherein your great strength lies." ¹⁶And when she pressed him hard with her words day after day, and urged him, his soul was vexed to death. ¹⁷And he told her all his mind, and said to her, "A razor has never come upon my head; for I have been a Naz′irite to God from my mother's womb. If I be shaved, then my strength will leave me, and I shall become weak, and be like any other man."

18 When Deli′lah saw that he had told her all his mind, she sent and called the lords of the Philis′tines, saying, "Come up this once, for he has told me all his mind." Then the lords of the Philistines came up to her, and brought the money in their hands. ¹⁹She made him sleep upon her knees; and she called a man, and had him shave off the seven locks of his head. Then she began to torment him, and his strength left him. ²⁰And she said, "The Philis′tines are upon you, Samson!" And he awoke from his sleep, and said, "I will go out as at other times, and shake myself free." And he did not know that the LORD had left him. ²¹And the Philis′tines seized him and gouged out his eyes, and brought him down to Gaza, and bound him with bronze fetters; and he ground at the mill in the prison. ²²But the hair of his head began to grow again after it had been shaved.

Samson's Death

23 Now the lords of the Philis′tines gathered to offer a great sacrifice to Da′gon their god, and to rejoice; for they said, "Our god has given Samson our enemy into our hand." ²⁴And when the people saw him, they praised their god; for they said, "Our god has given our enemy into our hand, the ravager of our country, who has slain many of us." ²⁵And when their hearts were merry, they said, "Call Samson, that he may make sport for us." So they called Samson out of the prison, and he made sport before them. They made him stand between the pillars; ²⁶and Samson said to the lad who held him by the hand, "Let me feel the pillars on which the house rests, that I may lean against them." ²⁷Now the house was full of men and women; all the lords of the Philis′tines were there, and on the roof there were about three thousand men and women, who looked on while Samson made sport.

28 Then Samson called to the LORD and said, "O Lord GOD, remember me, I beg you, and strengthen me, I beg you, only this once, O God, that I may be avenged upon the Philis′tines for one of my two eyes." ²⁹And Samson grasped the two middle pillars

---

16:13 weave the seven locks: Into an upright loom.

16:16 pressed him hard: Parallels the tenacious persistence of his wife in 14:17, to which he also succumbs after reaching a point of exasperation.

16:17 I have been a Nazirite: For the meaning of this, see note on 13:5.

16:20 the LORD had left him: Samson's physical strength is not in his hair but in his relationship with Yahweh, who has literally "turned away" from him (as he will turn from Saul in 1 Sam 28:15). Shaving off his hair was not the first violation of Samson's consecration, but it is the most conspicuous violation of his Nazirite way of life. The outward repudiation of his sanctity is thus met with an interior withdrawal of the Lord's gift of strength. • *Morally,* the spiritual plight of sinners may be compared to the bodily suffering of Samson. The enemy will mock us if we are stripped of the grace of Christ as Samson is shorn of his hair. Once a man slips from righteousness, he becomes like Samson, deprived of the strength of wisdom and grace, and he is consigned to the millstone of the beast because he makes himself an animal by serving his flesh (St. Paulinus of Nola, *Letters* 23, 12).

16:21 the mill: Samson is sentenced to the tedious labor of turning the stone grinder at the Gaza prison.

16:22 began to grow again: A small detail full of significance and expectation.

16:23 Dagon: Chief deity of the Philistines (1 Sam 5:2). He is revered as a god of fertility and grain, and in some mythological texts he is identified as the father of the Canaanite god Baal. **Our god has given:** Dagon, the grain god, is praised for the capture of Samson, who earlier had burned the Philistines' grainfields (15:5). Ironically, Samson's apprehension is arranged by the Providence of the God of Israel, who will use him to strike a devastating blow against the Philistines and their idol temple.

16:25 made sport: Onlookers revel in the spectacle of Samson's humiliation. **the pillars:** The remains of a Philistine sanctuary excavated at modern Tell Qasile have bases for twin pillars along the central axis of the building.

16:27 three thousand: The vastness of the crowd forebodes the scale of the tragedy that will follow when Samson causes the structure to collapse (16:30).

16:28 strengthen me: In weakness, Samson has come to realize that God is the source of his miraculous might. This is the second time in Judges that Samson is moved to prayer (the other is 15:18); both times, the Lord responds to his pleas with a miracle (15:19; 16:30). Acknowledging total dependence upon God is an expression of the faith for which Samson is remembered in the NT (Heb 11:32-34).

16:29 leaned: His herculean strength regained, Samson brings down the Philistine temple by pushing over its central supports. The Hebrew *samak* is often used in cultic contexts when a worshiper presses his hands on an animal designated

---

ʷCompare Gk: Heb lacks *and make it tight…into the web.*

upon which the house rested, and he leaned his weight upon them, his right hand on the one and his left hand on the other. ³⁰And Samson said, "Let me die with the Philis'tines." Then he bowed with all his might; and the house fell upon the lords and upon all the people that were in it. So the dead whom he slew at his death were more than those whom he had slain during his life. ³¹Then his brothers and all his family came down and took him and brought him up and buried him between Zorah and Esh'ta-ol in the tomb of Mano'ah his father. He had judged Israel twenty years.

Micah and the Levite

17 *There was a man of the hill country of E'phraim, whose name was Micah. ²And he said to his mother, "The eleven hundred pieces of silver which were taken from you, about which you uttered a curse, and also spoke it in my ears, behold, the silver is with me; I took it." And his mother said, "Blessed be my son by the Lord." ³And he restored the eleven hundred pieces of silver to his mother; and his mother said, "I consecrate the silver to the

Lord from my hand for my son, to make a graven image and a molten image; now therefore I will restore it to you." ⁴So when he restored the money to his mother, his mother took two hundred pieces of silver, and gave it to the silversmith, who made it into a graven image and a molten image; and it was in the house of Micah. ⁵And the man Micah had a shrine, and he made an ephod and teraphim, and installed one of his sons, who became his priest. ⁶In those days there was no king in Israel; every man did what was right in his own eyes.

7 Now there was a young man of Bethlehem in Judah, of the family of Judah, who was a Levite; and he sojourned there. ⁸And the man departed from the town of Bethlehem in Judah, to live where he could find a place; and as he journeyed, he came to the hill country of E'phraim to the house of Micah. ⁹And Micah said to him, "From where do you come?" And he said to him, "I am a Levite of Bethlehem in Judah, and I am going to sojourn where I may find a place." ¹⁰And Micah said to him, "Stay with me, and be to me a father

---

for sacrifice (Lev 1:4; 3:2, 8, etc.). Judges may be hinting that Samson's final act, resulting in the surrender of his life, is an acceptable offering to the Lord. See word study: *Lay* at Num 8:10.

16:30 death ... life: Samson fells more Philistines in this crowning moment than during his entire career as an unstoppable warrior. • *Allegorically*, the death of Samson prefigures the power of the Lord's Passion, by which the house of the devil caves in and the dominion of death is destroyed (St. Paulinus of Nola, *Letters* 23, 14). Just as Samson stretches forth his hands to the pillars and the house of the Philistines falls with its princes, so Christ extends his hands on the two beams of the Cross, overthrowing the house of the devil and his angels. The fact that more perish at his death than in his life signifies that few believe in Christ, the true Samson, before his crucifixion, but countless multitudes come under his doctrine afterward (St. Caesarius of Arles, *Sermons* 120).

16:31 Zorah: Samson's hometown (13:2). **twenty years:** The length of Samson's judgeship, also noted in 15:20. The Philistine oppression of Israel lasts twice as long (13:1).

17:1—21:25 The epilogue to Judges, which serves as a powerful exposé of the spiritual and moral chaos that prevail during these troubled times. If earlier chapters underscore the threat that foreign aggressors pose to Israel, these final chapters show that Israel is also threatened by internal disintegration and collapse from within. The epilogue consists of two accounts (chaps. 17–18 and 19–21), both of which feature an unnamed Levite who passes between Bethlehem and Ephraim. These final chapters are held together around the fourfold refrain: "In those days there was no king in Israel" (17:6; 18:1; 19:1; 21:25).

17:1—18:31 Judges 17–18 document the religious syncretism and cultic irregularities that plague Israel during the settlement period. The author brings out the scale of this crisis by implicating members of several different tribes—Ephraimites (17:1, 3, 5), a Levite (17:7), and virtually all of the Danites (18:1).

17:1 Ephraim: The tribe settled in central Canaan. **Micah:** A man of significant wealth but misguided in his piety. His name means "Who is like Yahweh?"

17:2 eleven hundred pieces: More than ten times the annual stipend offered to the Levite in 17:10. **Blessed be my son:** Intended to cancel the curse inadvertently spoken against her son, who took the silver.

17:3 to the Lord ... a graven image: The mother shows commendable devotion to Yahweh but appears to be ignorant of the Torah, which declares idol images incompatible with the worship of God (Ex 20:4; Deut 5:8). Her religion, like that of her son (17:5), is a mixture of Israelite concepts and Canaanite practices.

17:4 two hundred pieces: Note the discrepancy with the amount returned in 17:3.

17:5 ephod: Normally refers to a decorated vestment wore by the high priest of Israel (Ex 28:5–14), but here the reference may be to an idol (cf. Gideon's ephod in 8:27). **teraphim:** Or, "household gods" (Gen 31:19). They appear to have been cultic images or charms kept in private homes. **installed:** Literally, "filled the hand", an idiom for priestly ordination. See note on Ex 28:41. **one of his sons:** An Ephraimite and therefore ineligible for ministry according to the Mosaic Law, which makes priesthood the exclusive right of Aaron and his lineal descendants from the tribe of Levi (Ex 40:12–15).

17:6 no king in Israel: A refrain in the epilogue to Judges (18:1; 19:1; 21:25). **right in his own eyes:** For this statement, see note on 21:25.

17:7 Bethlehem: Five miles south of Jerusalem. **a Levite:** An unemployed clergyman from the tribe of Levi looking for a home and an income. He travels from Bethlehem to Ephraim (17:8) and takes a position as the chaplain-in-residence at Micah's family shrine (17:12). A greedy opportunist, he will soon abandon Micah to accept a more lucrative offer made by the Danites (18:19–20). For his identity, see 18:30.

17:10 a father and a priest: Priesthood is a cultic expression of fatherhood, as noted also in 18:19. This idea has its basis in biblical history: in the patriarchal period, before the natural family order gave way to the Mosaic legal order, fathers and patriarchs served as spiritual leaders over their families and presided over the rituals of public worship. The connection between "fathers" and "priests" is thus firmly rooted in Israel's sacred writings and traditions, as it also is in the conceptions of priesthood in the broader Near East. The NT bears witness to it in passages where the apostles view their ministry as a form of

---

*17–21: Extracts from tribal tradition which give a dark picture of the times.

and a priest, and I will give you ten pieces of silver a year, and a suit of apparel, and your living."ʷ² ¹¹And the Levite was content to dwell with the man; and the young man became to him like one of his sons. ¹²And Micah installed the Levite, and the young man became his priest, and was in the house of Micah. ¹³Then Micah said, "Now I know that the LORD will prosper me, because I have a Levite as priest."

Micah and the Migration of Dan

18 In those days there was no king in Israel. And in those days the tribe of the Da′nites was seeking for itself an inheritance to dwell in; for until then no inheritance among the tribes of Israel had fallen to them. ²So the Da′nites sent five able men from the whole number of their tribe, from Zorah and from Esh′ta-ol, to spy out the land and to explore it; and they said to them, "Go and explore the land." And they came to the hill country of E′phraim, to the house of Micah, and lodged there. ³When they were by the house of Micah, they recognized the voice of the young Levite; and they turned aside and said to him, "Who brought you here? What are you doing in this place? What is your business here?" ⁴And he said to them, "Thus and thus has Micah dealt with me: he has hired me, and I have become his priest." ⁵And they said to him, "Inquire of God, we beg you, that we may know whether the journey on which we are setting

out will succeed." ⁶And the priest said to them, "Go in peace. The journey on which you go is under the eye of the LORD."

7 Then the five men departed, and came to La′ish, and saw the people who were there, how they dwelt in security, after the manner of the Sido′nians, quiet and unsuspecting, lacking✗ nothing that is in the earth, and possessing wealth, and how they were far from the Sidonians and had no dealings with any one. ⁸And when they came to their brethren at Zorah and Esh′ta-ol, their brethren said to them, "What do you report?" ⁹They said, "Arise, and let us go up against them; for we have seen the land, and behold, it is very fertile. And will you do nothing? Do not be slow to go, and enter in and possess the land. ¹⁰When you go, you will come to an unsuspecting people. The land is broad; yes, God has given it into your hands, a place where there is no lack of anything that is in the earth."

11 And six hundred men of the tribe of Dan, armed with weapons of war, set forth from Zorah and Esh′ta-ol, ¹²and went up and encamped at Kir′iath-je′arim in Judah. On this account that place is called Ma′haneh-danʸ to this day; behold, it is west of Kiriath-jearim. ¹³And they passed on from there to the hill country of E′phraim, and came to the house of Micah.

14 Then the five men who had gone to spy out the country of La′ish said to their brethren,

---

18:7: Judg 18:27, 28.

---

spiritual, life-giving paternity (1 Cor 4:15; Phil 2:22; Tit 1:4; Philem 10). See essay: *Priesthood in the Old Testament* at Num 18. • As recently as Vatican II, the Church reasserted her belief that Catholic bishops and priests function as fathers and teachers of the People of God (*Lumen Gentium* 28; *Presbyterorum Ordinis* 9).

17:13 because I have a Levite: Micah has a vague sense that priests must be Levites, but he seems unaware that only Levites descended from Aaron are permitted to serve Israel in a priestly capacity. His confidence in gaining the Lord's blessing is thus ill-founded.

18:1–31 Judges 18 recounts the story of the Danite migration. Originally, the tribe of Dan is allotted a segment of coastland and hill country northwest of Jerusalem (Josh 19:40–46). However, the Danites are unable to secure the full extent of their land, owing to the tenacity of the Canaanites entrenched on the coastal plain (1:34). This leads them in search of conquerable territory in which the tribe can relocate. After spying out the land, they opt for a hostile takeover of the city of Laish on the northern frontier of Israel. No suggestion is made in the text of Judges that the Danite migration is based on a divine mandate or is divinely approved (the statement in 18:6 being illegitimate). The undertaking is a purely human affair driven by human calculations and actions.

18:1 no king in Israel: A refrain in the epilogue to Judges (17:6; 19:1; 21:25).

18:2 Zorah: Samson's hometown. See note on 13:2. **spy out the land:** An effort to gather military intelligence in prepa-

ration for an attack. Earlier missions of this sort were ordered by Moses (Num 13:1–24) and Joshua (Josh 2:1–24).

18:3 recognized the voice: The Levite speaks with a southern, Judahite accent or perhaps in a southern, Judahite dialect. **the young Levite:** Introduced in 17:7–8.

18:7 Laish: Archaeologically identified with modern Tell Dan, near the source of the Jordan River over 100 miles north of Dan's original land assignment. The town was called "Leshem" (Josh 19:47) before the Israelite conquerors rename it "Dan" (18:29). The date of the Danite conquest of Laish is uncertain, but archaeological evidence points to a change in occupation around the beginning of the Iron Age (1200 B.C.). The Danite spies describe it as a fertile and well-situated place, where the inhabitants live peacefully and prosperously (18:9–10). **Sidonians:** Residents of the port city of Sidon on the Mediterranean coast of Phoenicia. **no dealings with any one:** Laish has formed no alliances with other city-states (18:28). This leaves the city isolated from military assistance and vulnerable to the designs of the Danites.

18:12 Kiriath-jearim: A border town of Judah roughly eight miles northwest of Jerusalem (Josh 18:14). **Mahaneh-dan:** Means "camp of Dan". The location is commemorated as an initial staging point for Dan's fateful assault on Laish.

18:13 hill country of Ephraim: In central Canaan.

18:14–20 Six hundred Danites rob Micah of his idols and his chaplain on their northward march through Ephraimite territory. Their thievery may be seen as an instance of poetic justice: Micah, who stole a cache of silver from his mother (17:2), is burglarized of the idol that was made from this silver (17:4), along with his priest, who was paid for his services from the same lot of silver (17:10).

18:14 ephod ... teraphim ... image: Cultic items installed in Micah's home and shrine. See note on 17:5.

ʷ²Heb *living, and the Levite went.*
✗Cn Compare 18:10. The Hebrew text is uncertain.
ʸThat is *Camp of Dan.*

"Do you know that in these houses there are an ephod, teraphim, a graven image, and a molten image? Now therefore consider what you will do." ¹⁵And they turned aside there, and came to the house of the young Levite, at the home of Micah, and asked him of his welfare. ¹⁶Now the six hundred men of the Da′nites, armed with their weapons of war, stood by the entrance of the gate; ¹⁷and the five men who had gone to spy out the land went up, and entered and took the graven image, the ephod, the teraphim, and the molten image, while the priest stood by the entrance of the gate with the six hundred men armed with weapons of war. ¹⁸And when these went into Micah's house and took the graven image, the ephod, the teraphim, and the molten image, the priest said to them, "What are you doing?" ¹⁹And they said to him, "Keep quiet, put your hand upon your mouth, and come with us, and be to us a father and a priest. Is it better for you to be priest to the house of one man, or to be priest to a tribe and family in Israel?" ²⁰And the priest's heart was glad; he took the ephod, and the teraphim, and the graven image, and went in the midst of the people.

21 So they turned and departed, putting the little ones and the cattle and the goods in front of them. ²²When they were a good way from the home of Micah, the men who were in the houses near Micah's house were called out, and they overtook the Da′nites. ²³And they shouted to the Da′nites, who turned round and said to Micah, "What ails you that you come with such a company?" ²⁴And he said, "You take my gods which I made, and the priest, and go away, and what have I left? How then do you ask me, 'What ails you?'" ²⁵And the Da′nites said to him, "Do not let your voice be heard among us, lest angry fellows fall upon you, and you lose your life with the lives of your household." ²⁶Then the Da′nites went their way; and when Micah saw that they were too strong for him, he turned and went back to his home.

The Danites Settle in Laish

27 And taking what Micah had made, and the priest who belonged to him, the Da′nites came to La′ish, to a people quiet and unsuspecting, and struck them with the edge of the sword, and burned the city with fire. ²⁸And there was no deliverer because it was far from Si′don, and they had no dealings with any one. It was in the valley which belongs to Beth-re′hob. And they rebuilt the city, and dwelt in it. ²⁹And they named the city Dan, after the name of Dan their ancestor, who was born to Israel; but the name of the city was La′ish at the first. ³⁰And the Da′nites set up the graven image for themselves; and Jonathan the son of Gershom, son of Moses,ᶻ and his sons were priests to the tribe of the Da′nites until the day of the captivity of the land. ³¹So they set up Micah's graven image which he made, as long as the house of God was at Shiloh.

18:19 a father and a priest: For the significance of this, see note on 17:10. **be priest to a tribe:** Better circumstances, from the standpoint of financial gain and personal well-being, than what was provided by Micah (17:10).

18:21 in front of them: To protect livestock and children from a rear attack by pursuing Ephraimites.

18:24 my gods which I made: An obvious deviation from Israel's faith. The Decalogue forbids the covenant people both to recognize "other gods" and to "make" graven images for worship (Ex 20:3-4; Deut 5:7-8). See note on Ex 20:4.

18:25 lest ... you lose your life: Micah is threatened with a merciless counterattack.

18:27 Laish: See note on 18:7.

18:28 valley ... Beth-rehob: Perhaps a reference to the Beqa′ Valley more broadly.

18:29 Dan their ancestor: The patriarch Dan, fifth son of Jacob/Israel by Rachel's maid, Bilhah (Gen 30:3-6).

📖 **18:30 set up the graven image:** Dan is made the center of an idolatrous cult and an illegitimate priesthood. • Transfer of the idol and priest from Ephraim to Dan anticipates the religious rebellion of the northern Kingdom of Israel, which in later centuries installs images of a golden calf, one in Dan and the other in Bethel in the hill country of Ephraim, along with priests ineligible for the office (1 Kings 12:26-31). **Jonathan:** The identity of the unnamed Levite (17:7), who is hired first by Micah (17:10) and then by the tribe of Dan (18:19), is finally revealed: He is the grandson (or "descendant") of Moses in the line of his firstborn son, **Gershom** (Ex 2:22). Judges draws a sharp contrast between Jonathan, the grandson of Moses, who conducts unlawful priestly service before idols, and Phinehas, the grandson of Aaron, who ministers as Israel's legitimate high priest before the Ark of the Covenant (20:28). **Moses:** The name that appears in most ancient versions. An exception is the Hebrew text (MT), which has the name "Manasseh" instead. Some scholars conjecture that the name Moses was changed by a later scribe to read Manasseh, given the scandalous association of Jonathan and his sons with idolatry. Only a single letter differentiates the spelling of the two names in the Hebrew text, which consists solely of consonants. **until the day of the captivity:** A chronological note of uncertain meaning. **(1)** It may be a reference to the Assyrian conquest of northern Palestine by Tiglath Pileser III in 734 B.C. (2 Kings 15:29). Captivity, in this case, would refer to the forcible removal of the people from their homeland. **(2)** Alternatively, it may be a reference to the Philistine conquest of Shiloh in the eleventh century B.C. (1 Sam 4-6). Captivity, in this case, would refer to the confiscation of the Ark of the Covenant from the sanctuary at Shiloh (Ps 78:60-61). In favor of the former, the captivity would have a direct bearing on the land occupied by Dan; in favor of the latter, the very next verse seems to bring this event into close connection with the history of the Shiloh temple.

18:31 Shiloh: Ten miles north of Bethel in central Canaan. Israel's sanctuary was stationed in Shiloh in the days of Joshua (Josh 18:1) but was later overrun by the Philistines in the days of Samuel (1 Sam 4:10-11). Archaeology attests the destruction of Shiloh in the middle of the eleventh century.

ᶻ Another reading is *Manasseh*.

The Levite's Concubine

19 In those days, when there was no king in Israel, a certain Levite was sojourning in the remote parts of the hill country of E'phraim, who took to himself a concubine from Bethlehem in Judah. [2] And his concubine became angry with[a] him, and she went away from him to her father's house at Bethlehem in Judah, and was there some four months. [3] Then her husband arose and went after her, to speak kindly to her and bring her back. He had with him his servant and a couple of donkeys. And he came[b] to her father's house; and when the girl's father saw him, he came with joy to meet him. [4] And his father-in-law, the girl's father, made him stay, and he remained with him three days; so they ate and drank, and lodged there. [5] And on the fourth day they arose early in the morning, and he prepared to go; but the girl's father said to his son-in-law, "Strengthen your heart with a morsel of bread, and after that you may go." [6] So the two men sat and ate and drank together; and the girl's father said to the man, "Be pleased to spend the night, and let your heart be merry." [7] And when the man rose up to go, his father-in-law urged him, till he lodged there again. [8] And on the fifth day he arose early in the morning to depart; and the girl's father said, "Strengthen your heart, and tarry until the day declines." So they ate, both of them. [9] And when the man and his concubine and his servant rose up to depart, his father-in-law, the girl's father, said to him, "Behold, now the day has waned toward evening; please tarry all night. Behold, the day draws to its close; lodge here and let your heart be merry; and tomorrow you shall arise early in the morning for your journey, and go home."

10 But the man would not spend the night; he rose up and departed, and arrived opposite Je'bus (that is, Jerusalem). He had with him a couple of saddled donkeys, and his concubine was with him. [11] When they were near Je'bus, the day was far spent, and the servant said to his master, "Come now, let us turn aside to this city of the Jeb'usites, and spend the night in it." [12] And his master said to him, "We will not turn aside into the city of foreigners, who do not belong to the sons of Israel; but we will pass on to Gib'e-ah." [13] And he said to his servant, "Come and let us draw near to one of these places, and spend the night at Gib'e-ah or at Ra'mah." [14] So they passed on and went their way; and the sun went down on them near Gib'e-ah, which belongs to Benjamin, [15] and they turned aside there, to go in and spend the night at Gib'e-ah. And he went in and sat down in the open square of the city; for no man took them into his house to spend the night.

16 And behold, an old man was coming from his work in the field at evening; the man was from the hill country of E'phraim, and he was sojourning in Gib'e-ah; the men of the place were Benjaminites. [17] And he lifted up his eyes, and saw the wayfarer in the open square of the city; and the old man said, "Where are you going? and from where do you come?" [18] And he said to him, "We are passing from Bethlehem in Judah to the remote parts of the hill country of E'phraim, from which I come. I went to Bethlehem in Judah; and I am going to my home;[c] and nobody takes me into his house. [19] We have straw and food for our donkeys, with bread and wine for me and your maidservant and the young man with your servants; there is no lack of anything." [20] And the old man said, "Peace be to you; I will care for all your wants; only, do not spend the night in the square." [21] So he brought him into his house, and fed the donkeys; and they washed their feet, and ate and drank.

19:1—21:25 The final chapters in Judges tell a story of moral outrage leading to civil war. The finger of blame is thrust at the tribe of Benjamin, whose inhospitality (19:14–15) and sexual depravity call to mind the ancient Sodomites (19:16–26). As a consequence of their actions, they are attacked by the other tribes of Israel (19:29–48) and barely escape total annihilation (21:16–24).

19:1 no king in Israel: A refrain in the epilogue to Judges (17:6; 18:1; 21:25). **a certain Levite:** An unnamed sojourner dwelling in Ephraimite territory in the highlands of central Israel. He is not the Levite Jonathan from the preceding story (17:7; 18:30). **concubine:** A wife of lower social and legal rank than a primary wife, whose children would be the main beneficiaries of a father's inheritance (Gen 25:5–6). Still, the girl's father is identified as the Levite's "father-in-law" (19:4). **Bethlehem:** Five miles south of Jerusalem in Judahite territory.

19:2 angry with him: The reason, according to the LXX, why the woman walks out on her husband. The Hebrew says

that she is maritally unfaithful, but this seems less congruent with the story.

19:4 made him stay: Polite but insistent appeals are characteristic of oriental hospitality. The zealous and extravagant reception of the Levite in Bethlehem stands in glaring contrast to the dreadful reception he and his company are soon to receive in Gibeah (19:14–26). For the political significance of this in Israel's history, see introduction: *Author and Date.*

19:9 please tarry all night: The reason for delaying their departure yet again is uncertain, but its effect is comical.

19:10 Jebus: A name sometimes given to Jerusalem when it was still occupied by Jebusites, one of the non-Israelite inhabitants of Canaan (1 Chron 11:4). Perhaps dissuaded by fear, the Levite refuses to seek accommodations in a "city of foreigners" (19:12). See note on 1:8.

19:14 Gibe-ah: Five miles north of Jerusalem in Benjaminite territory. Owing in part to the awful events in 19:22–26, it acquires a reputation for shameful iniquity (Hos 9:9). Gibeah is also remembered in the Bible as the hometown and command center of Israel's first king, Saul of Benjamin (1 Sam 10:26).

19:15 sat down in the open square: Advertising their need for overnight lodging.

---

[a] Gk Old Latin: Heb *played the harlot against.*
[b] Gk: Heb *she brought him.*
[c] Gk Compare 19:29. Heb *to the house of the* LORD.

The Crime of the Benjaminites of Gibe-ah

22 As they were making their hearts merry, behold, the men of the city, base fellows, surrounded the house, beating on the door; and they said to the old man, the master of the house, "Bring out the man who came into your house, that we may know him." ²³And the man, the master of the house, went out to them and said to them, "No, my brethren, do not act so wickedly; seeing that this man has come into my house, do not do this vile thing. ²⁴Behold, here are my virgin daughter and his concubine; let me bring them out now. Ravish them and do with them what seems good to you; but against this man do not do so vile a thing." ²⁵But the men would not listen to him. So the man seized his concubine, and put her out to them; and they knew her, and abused her all night until the morning. And as the dawn began to break, they let her go. ²⁶And as morning appeared, the woman came and fell down at the door of the man's house where her master was, till it was light.

27 And her master rose up in the morning, and when he opened the doors of the house and went out to go on his way, behold, there was his concubine lying at the door of the house, with her hands on the threshold. ²⁸He said to her, "Get up, let us be going."

But there was no answer. Then he put her upon the donkey; and the man rose up and went away to his home. ²⁹And when he entered his house, he took a knife, and laying hold of his concubine he divided her, limb by limb, into twelve pieces, and sent her throughout all the territory of Israel. ³⁰And all who saw it said, "Such a thing has never happened or been seen from the day that the sons of Israel came up out of the land of Egypt until this day; consider it, take counsel, and speak."

The Tribes of Israel Attack the Benjaminites

20 Then all the sons of Israel came out, from Dan to Be′er-she′ba, including the land of Gilead, and the congregation assembled as one man to the Lord at Mizpah. ²And the chiefs of all the people, of all the tribes of Israel, presented themselves in the assembly of the people of God, four hundred thousand men on foot that drew the sword. ³(Now the Benjaminites heard that the sons of Israel had gone up to Mizpah.) And the sons of Israel said, "Tell us, how was this wickedness brought to pass?" ⁴And the Levite, the husband of the woman who was murdered, answered and said, "I came to Gib′e-ah that belongs to Benjamin, I and my concubine, to spend the night. ⁵And the

---

19:22–26 Gibe-ah turns against its guests and commits monstrous crimes against them. Not only do these Benjaminites violate the ethics of hospitality, failing to offer them shelter, but they reveal their extreme depravity through acts of homosexual lust, gang rape, and lethal violence (CCC 2268, 2351, 2356–57). • Multiple parallels indicate that the men of Gibe-ah have become indistinguishable from the men of Sodom. The lodging of strangers, the nighttime setting, the clamor of the gathering mob, the demand to "know" the visitors in a perverse sexual way, and the substitution of innocent women for the male guests—all combine to show that Gibe-ah is reenacting the abominations of Sodom in Gen 19:1–11.

19:22 base fellows: Literally, "sons of Belial". In later Judaism, Belial is used as an epithet for Satan. An alternative form, Beliar, appears with this meaning in 2 Cor 6:15.

19:24 daughter ... concubine: Hardly a morally acceptable offer. Rejection of the offer only accentuates the townsmen's disordered preference for men over women.

19:28 Get up, let us be going: The Levite shows an appalling lack of compassion for his concubine, and the author gives no hint that he is saddened or distraught by the savage abuse

she has suffered. His only visible emotion, implied in 19:29, is anger. **no answer:** The woman is already dead. The author of Judges will say she was "murdered" (20:4).

19:29 divided her ... sent her: A ghastly deed that functions as a call to arms, as indicated by the similar action of Saul in 1 Sam 11:6–8. It is meant to kindle the fires of outrage and create a unified front against the men of Gibeah.

20:1 Dan to Beer-sheba: Cities near the northern and southern extremities of Israelite territory. This is a stock expression for the whole land of Israel west of the Jordan (1 Sam 3:20; 2 Sam 24:15; etc.). **Gilead:** Israelite territory east of the Jordan. **as one man:** Despite intertribal tensions and conflicts throughout the period of the judges, there remains a sense that Israel is still a unified nation, a tribal family of brethren (20:13; 21:6). **Mizpah:** A few miles north of Gibeah near the border between Ephraim and Benjamin (different from the Mizpah in 10:17). It will serve as a place of assembly also in 1 Sam 7:5–6.

20:5 meant to kill me: Murderous intent is not mentioned in the account in 19:22 but may be inferred from the death of the woman subjected to their cruelty (19:27–28).

WORD STUDY

Know (19:22)

yada‘ (Heb.): a verb meaning "know", "perceive", or "become acquainted with". In Hebrew thinking, a person comes to possess knowledge by thoughtful reflection, divine revelation, or direct experience. To know intellectually is to understand something with the mind (Eccles 1:17). To know experientially is to have intimate involvement with someone or to live through something and derive a lesson from it. In Scripture, knowing the Lord means having a close personal relationship built on faith and trust (Ps 9:10; Is 43:10). People can come to know God by his self-revelation (Ex 33:13), his covenant promises (Gen 15:8–21), his mighty deeds (Ex 10:2), or even by experiencing his discipline (Deut 8:5) and judgment (Ezek 25:14; Hos 9:7). In several passages, the verb functions as a euphemism for sexual intimacy. A husband knows his wife in the marital embrace (Gen 4:1), and a virgin, by definition, is one who has never experienced sexual involvement with another (Gen 24:16; Judg 21:12). Knowing in this sense is gravely sinful when it takes the form of rape (Judg 19:25) and homosexual acts (Gen 19:5; Judg 19:22).

men of Gib'e-ah rose against me, and surrounded the house by night; they meant to kill me, and they ravished my concubine, and she is dead. ⁶And I took my concubine and cut her in pieces, and sent her throughout all the country of the inheritance of Israel; for they have committed abomination and wantonness in Israel. ⁷Behold, you sons of Israel, all of you, give your advice and counsel here."

8 And all the people arose as one man, saying, "None of us will go to his tent, and none of us will return to his house. ⁹But now this is what we will do to Gib'e-ah: we will go up against it by lot, ¹⁰and we will take ten men of a hundred throughout all the tribes of Israel, and a hundred of a thousand, and a thousand of ten thousand, to bring provisions for the people, that when they come they may repay Gib'e-ah of Benjamin, for all the wanton crime which they have committed in Israel." ¹¹So all the men of Israel gathered against the city, united as one man.

12 And the tribes of Israel sent men through all the tribe of Benjamin, saying, "What wickedness is this that has taken place among you? ¹³Now therefore give up the men, the base fellows in Gib'e-ah, that we may put them to death, and put away evil from Israel." But the Benjaminites would not listen to the voice of their brethren, the sons of Israel. ¹⁴And the Benjaminites came together out of the cities to Gib'e-ah, to go out to battle against the sons of Israel. ¹⁵And the Benjaminites mustered out of their cities on that day twenty-six thousand men that drew the sword, besides the inhabitants of Gib'e-ah, who mustered seven hundred picked men. ¹⁶Among all these were seven hundred picked men who were left-handed; every one could sling a stone at a hair, and not miss. ¹⁷And the men of Israel, apart from Benjamin, mustered four

hundred thousand men that drew sword; all these were men of war.

18 The sons of Israel arose and went up to Bethel, and inquired of God, "Which of us shall go up first to battle against the Benjaminites?" And the LORD said, "Judah shall go up first."

19 Then the sons of Israel rose in the morning, and encamped against Gib'e-ah. ²⁰And the men of Israel went out to battle against Benjamin; and the men of Israel drew up the battle line against them at Gib'e-ah. ²¹The Benjaminites came out of Gib'e-ah, and struck down on that day twenty-two thousand men of the Israelites. ²²But the people, the men of Israel, took courage, and again formed the battle line in the same place where they had formed it on the first day. ²³And the sons of Israel went up and wept before the LORD until the evening; and they inquired of the LORD, "Shall we again draw near to battle against our brethren the Benjaminites?" And the LORD said, "Go up against them."

24 So the sons of Israel came near against the Benjaminites the second day. ²⁵And Benjamin went against them out of Gib'e-ah the second day, and struck down eighteen thousand men of the sons of Israel; all these were men who drew the sword. ²⁶Then all the sons of Israel, the whole army, went up and came to Bethel and wept; they sat there before the LORD, and fasted that day until evening, and offered burnt offerings and peace offerings before the LORD. ²⁷And the sons of Israel inquired of the LORD (for the ark of the covenant of God was there in those days, ²⁸and Phin'ehas the son of Elea'zar, son of Aaron, ministered before it in those days), saying, "Shall we yet again go out to battle against our brethren the Benjaminites, or shall we cease?" And the LORD said, "Go up; for tomorrow I will give them into your hand."

20:9 we will go up against it: The coalition will make a show of force in Gibeah, with the aim of putting the perpetrators of the crime to death (20:13). But Benjamin's refusal to hand the criminals over to justice (20:13) escalates the confrontation into civil war (20:14). Battle ensues between 26,700 swordsmen and slingers from Benjamin and 400,000 armed warriors enlisted from the other tribes (20:19–48). For a discussion of large numbers in the Bible, see note on Num 1:46.
20:16 left-handed: A peculiar trait among the Benjaminites (3:15). Ironically, the Hebrew name Benjamin means "son of the right hand".
20:18 Bethel: A few miles north of Mizpah and Gibeah. The city at this time is host to the Ark of the Covenant as well as the high priest, Phinehas (20:27–28). Most likely the Ark was transferred to Bethel from the sanctuary in Shiloh (Josh 18:1), to which it will later return (1 Sam 1:3). Bethel has been a sacred site since patriarchal times (Gen 28:18–22; 35:6–7). **inquired:** By means of the sacred lots, the Urim and Thummim, which are kept in the custody of the high priest (Ex 28:30; Num 27:21). **Judah:** Chosen to lead the attack against the Benjaminites, just as the same tribe was chosen to make the first strike against the Canaanites (1:1–2). The selection is logical, since the woman who was raped and killed was from Bethlehem in Judah (19:1).
20:19–48 Israel's war against Benjamin. The multitribal army suffers heavy casualties and unexpected setbacks on the

first two days of battle (20:19–28), finally to win a smashing victory on the third day (20:29–48).
20:23 went up and wept: Before the Ark of the Covenant in Bethel (as in 20:18, 26–27).
20:25 eighteen thousand: The casualty count reaches 40,000 soldiers after two days of battle (20:21), equal to one-tenth of the Israelite forces mustered (20:17). This is evidence of covenant solidarity in Israel: the sin of one tribe brings some suffering to all the tribes.
20:27 the ark of the covenant: Represents the throne of Yahweh (Is 37:16) as well as his battle chariot (1 Chron 28:18). Perhaps it is installed in a temporary tent in Bethel, just as David would do in Jerusalem (2 Sam 6:17). For the shape and dimensions of the Ark, see notes on Ex 25:10 and 25:18. **inquired:** See note on 20:18.
20:28 Phinehas: Grandson of Aaron, the brother of Moses (Ex 6:25), who is awarded a covenant of perpetual priesthood for his zealous defense of the Torah (Num 25:7–11). He is the lawful high priest of Israel, in contrast to the illegitimate priest Jonathan, the grandson of Moses who ministers to the Danites (18:30). The appearance of Phinehas in the account indicates that the civil war against Benjamin must have taken place very early in the period of the judges, when he was ministering to the tribes newly settled in Canaan (Josh 22:13). **Eleazar:** Aaron's first successor as high priest (Deut 10:6).

29 So Israel set men in ambush round about Gib′e-ah. ³⁰And the sons of Israel went up against the Benjaminites on the third day, and set themselves in array against Gib′e-ah, as at other times. ³¹And the Benjaminites went out against the people, and were drawn away from the city; and as at other times they began to strike and kill some of the people, in the highways, one of which goes up to Bethel and the other to Gib′e-ah, and in the open country, about thirty men of Israel. ³²And the Benjaminites said, "They are routed before us, as at the first." But the men of Israel said, "Let us flee, and draw them away from the city to the highways." ³³And all the men of Israel rose up out of their place, and set themselves in array at Ba′al-ta′mar; and the men of Israel who were in ambush rushed out of their place west ᵈ of Ge′ba. ³⁴And there came against Gib′e-ah ten thousand picked men out of all Israel, and the battle was hard; but the Benjaminites did not know that disaster was close upon them. ³⁵And the Lᴏʀᴅ defeated Benjamin before Israel; and the men of Israel destroyed twenty-five thousand one hundred men of Benjamin that day; all these were men who drew the sword. ³⁶So the Benjaminites saw that they were defeated.

The men of Israel gave ground to Benjamin, because they trusted to the men in ambush whom they had set against Gib′e-ah. ³⁷And the men in ambush made haste and rushed upon Gib′e-ah; the men in ambush moved out and struck the whole city with the edge of the sword. ³⁸Now the appointed signal between the men of Israel and the men in ambush was that when they made a great cloud of smoke rise up out of the city ³⁹the men of Israel should turn in battle. Now Benjamin had begun to strike and kill about thirty men of Israel; they said, "Surely they are struck down before us, as in the first battle." ⁴⁰But when the signal began to rise out of the city in a column of smoke, the Benjaminites looked behind them; and behold, the whole city went up in smoke to heaven. ⁴¹Then the men of Israel turned, and the men of Benjamin were dismayed, for they saw that disaster was close upon them. ⁴²Therefore they turned their backs before the men of Israel in the direction of the wilderness; but the battle overtook them, and those who came out of the cities destroyed them in the midst of them. ⁴³Cutting down ᵉ the Benjaminites, they pursued them and trod them down from No′hah ᶠ as far as opposite Gib′e-ah on the east. ⁴⁴Eighteen thousand men of Benjamin fell, all of them men of valor. ⁴⁵And they turned and fled toward the wilderness to the rock of Rimmon; five thousand men of them were cut down in the highways, and they were pursued hard to Gi′dom, and two thousand men of them were slain. ⁴⁶So all who fell that day of Benjamin were twenty-five thousand men that drew the sword, all of them men of valor. ⁴⁷But six hundred men turned and fled toward the wilderness to the rock of Rimmon, and abode at the rock of Rimmon four months. ⁴⁸And the men of Israel turned back against the Benjaminites, and struck them with the edge of the sword, men and beasts and all that they found. And all the towns which they found they set on fire.

The Benjaminites Saved from Extinction

21 Now the men of Israel had sworn at Mizpah, "No one of us shall give his daughter in marriage to Benjamin." ²And the people came to Bethel, and sat there till evening before God, and they lifted up their voices and wept bitterly. ³And they said, "O Lᴏʀᴅ, the God of Israel, why has this come to pass in Israel, that there should be today one tribe lacking in Israel?" ⁴And the next day the people rose early, and built there an altar, and offered burnt offerings and peace offerings. ⁵And

---

20:29–48 Benjamin is systematically routed and reduced to a tiny remnant of 600 soldiers (20:47). Triumph is achieved by a strategy of diversion and ambush, reminiscent of the overthrow of Ai in Josh 8:1–29. The account is difficult to follow in places because the author alternates between the perspective of the Israelites and that of the Benjaminites.

20:33 Baal-tamar ... Geba: Close to Gibeah but exact locations unknown.

20:35 the Lᴏʀᴅ defeated Benjamin: Just as the oracle in 20:28 predicted. The idea is that Benjamin's defeat is the enactment of divine judgment for sin. Yahweh is often depicted as a divine Warrior, fighting against Israel's enemies; in this case, however, the enemy is present within Israel.

20:40 went up in smoke: The sight of Gibeah burning and billowing smoke recalls Abraham's vision of Sodom and Gomorrah after fire fell on the wicked cities (Gen 19:27–29). Having repeated the crimes of Sodom, Gibeah shares the fate of Sodom. For the parallels between the two cities, see note on 19:22–26.

20:45 the rock of Rimmon: Means "Pomegranate Rock". It is often identified with a large cave more than two miles east of Gibeah. **Gidom:** Location unknown.

20:47 six hundred men: All that is left of Benjamin's 26,700 fighters (20:15).

20:48 set on fire: Towns set ablaze will be rebuilt by Benjaminite survivors (21:23).

21:1–24 Israel's massacre of the Benjaminites is so severe that it pushes the tribe to the brink of extinction. This gives rise to a new dilemma: only 600 spouseless men survive the campaign, so unless wives can be procured for them, Benjamin will die off within a generation. Complicating the crisis, the other tribes of Israel swear an oath not to give their daughters in marriage to the Benjaminites. The assembly resorts to a strange but creative solution: 400 unmarried girls are seized as conquerors' spoil from Jabesh-gilead (21:8–15), and another 200 are abducted from the festival dances at Shiloh (21:16–24). Neither tactic is commanded or explicitly approved by the Lord.

21:1 Mizpah: Where the tribal gathering initially takes place (see 20:1). **give his daughter:** The whole tribal family of Israel has sworn an oath to refuse intermarriage with Benjamin under the threat of a curse (see 21:18).

21:2 Bethel: See note on 20:18. **sat ... before God:** I.e., in front of the Ark of the Covenant, as in 20:26–27.

21:5 He shall be put to death: The words of a second oath sworn at Mizpah, this one to destroy utterly those Israelites who fail to join the coalition against Benjamin.

ᵈ Gk Vg: Heb *in the plain.*
ᵉ Gk: Heb *surrounding.*
ᶠ Gk: Heb (*at their*) *resting place.*

the sons of Israel said, "Which of all the tribes of Israel did not come up in the assembly to the LORD?" For they had taken a great oath concerning him who did not come up to the LORD to Mizpah, saying, "He shall be put to death." ⁶And the sons of Israel had compassion for Benjamin their brother, and said, "One tribe is cut off from Israel this day. ⁷What shall we do for wives for those who are left, since we have sworn by the LORD that we will not give them any of our daughters for wives?"

8 And they said, "What one is there of the tribes of Israel that did not come up to the LORD to Mizpah?" And behold, no one had come to the camp from Ja'besh-gil'ead, to the assembly. ⁹For when the people were mustered, behold, not one of the inhabitants of Ja'besh-gil'ead was there. ¹⁰So the congregation sent twelve thousand of their bravest men there, and commanded them, "Go and strike the inhabitants of Ja'besh-gil'ead with the edge of the sword; also the women and the little ones. ¹¹This is what you shall do; every male and every woman that has lain with a male you shall utterly destroy." ¹²And they found among the inhabitants of Ja'besh-gil'ead four hundred young virgins who had not known man by lying with him; and they brought them to the camp at Shiloh, which is in the land of Canaan.

13 Then the whole congregation sent word to the Benjaminites who were at the rock of Rimmon, and proclaimed peace to them. ¹⁴And Benjamin returned at that time; and they gave them the women whom they had saved alive of the women of Ja'besh-gil'ead; but they did not suffice for them. ¹⁵And the people had compassion on Benjamin because the LORD had made a breach in the tribes of Israel.

16 Then the elders of the congregation said, "What shall we do for wives for those who are left, since the women are destroyed out of Benjamin?" ¹⁷And they said, "There must be an inheritance for the survivors of Benjamin, that a tribe be not blotted out from Israel. ¹⁸Yet we cannot give them wives of our daughters." For the sons of Israel had sworn, "Cursed be he who gives a wife to Benjamin." ¹⁹So they said, "Behold, there is the yearly feast of the LORD at Shiloh, which is north of Bethel, on the east of the highway that goes up from Bethel to She'chem, and south of Lebo'nah." ²⁰And they commanded the Benjaminites, saying, "Go and lie in wait in the vineyards, ²¹and watch; if the daughters of Shiloh come out to dance in the dances, then come out of the vineyards and seize each man his wife from the daughters of Shiloh, and go to the land of Benjamin. ²²And when their fathers or their brothers come to complain to us, we will say to them, 'Grant them graciously to us; because we did not take for each man of them his wife in battle, neither did you give them to them, else you would now be guilty.'" ²³And the Benjaminites did so, and took their wives, according to their number, from the dancers whom they carried off; then they went and returned to their inheritance, and rebuilt the towns, and dwelt in them. ²⁴And the sons of Israel departed from there at that time, every man to his tribe and family, and they went out from there every man to his inheritance.

25 In those days there was no king in Israel; every man did what was right in his own eyes.

21:8 Jabesh-gilead: A settlement east of the Jordan River, its precise location uncertain. It represents a legal loophole in the sworn pledges made at Mizpah. On the one hand, this town never took the oath to refuse intermarriage with Benjamin (21:1); on the other, it fell under the oath promising death to non-participants in the tribal meeting (21:5). Jabesh-gilead thus becomes a target of military action as well as a place from which to obtain wives for the surviving Benjaminites.

21:11 utterly destroy: A reference to *ḥerem* warfare, on which, see word study: *Devoted* at Josh 6:17.

21:12 young virgins: For a similar campaign, where Israel wars against the Midianites but takes their unmarried women captive, see Num 31:1–18. **Shiloh:** See note on 18:31.

21:13 the rock of Rimmon: See note on 20:45.

21:16–24 A follow-up plan is devised to meet the quota of wives still needed for the 200 Benjaminites without spouses. Again, a rationalizing logic evades the predicament of the oath sworn at Mizpah in 21:1: the daughters of Israel cannot be *given* to the Benjaminites, lest the oath be violated, but nothing prevents the Benjaminites from *taking* young maidens of their choice.

21:17 inheritance: Benjamin's lands must remain a Benjaminite possession; however, this cannot be realized unless the tribe is able to regrow its population.

21:19 feast of the LORD: An annual festival celebrated with dancing girls, the "daughters of Shiloh" (21:21). Some envision a local religious feast about which nothing further is known. Others envision one of Israel's national festivals, perhaps the pilgrim Feast of Booths (later called Tabernacles), which occurs every autumn at the close of the harvest season (Deut 16:13–17). That the celebration takes place in **Shiloh** is significant, since this is where the Lord's sanctuary is stationed at the time (18:31; Josh 18:1).

21:25 no king in Israel: A refrain in the epilogue to Judges (17:6; 18:1; 19:1) having several layers of significance. **(1)** *Historically*, the comment appears to be retrospective, the author looking back from a time when kingship was an established institution in Israel. **(2)** *Canonically*, the book concludes on this note to prepare for the next major development in the biblical story: the founding of the Israelite monarchy (1 Sam 8–10). **(3)** *Politically*, the remark implicitly contrasts the stability of the monarchical period with the instability that plagued the era of the judges. From the author's perspective, monarchy represents at least a partial solution to the problem of social and religious anarchy in Israel. **(4)** *Theologically*, the author is no less aware that kingship represents only a partial solution, since Israel's dilemma has more to do with sin than with a lack of centralized government. This is clearly indicated in the book's prologue (especially 2:11–23). **what was right in his own eyes:** A way of saying that relativism reigned supreme in the days of the judges. It was a time when the law of individual preference had a firmer hold on the masses than the law of God. • The expression recalls Deut 12:8, where Moses warns against "every man doing whatever is right in his own eyes". It would seem that liturgical abuses and disorder are primarily (but not exclusively) in view, since this warning serves as a preface to the law of the central sanctuary in Deut 12:10–11. Later on, David will rise above the chaos of the times by doing what is "right in the eyes of the LORD" (1 Kings 15:5).

STUDY QUESTIONS

Chapter 1

For understanding
1. **1:1—2:5.** How does the Book of Judges open? What success do the northern tribes and the tribes of Judah, Simeon, Joseph, and Benjamin have in subduing Canaan?
2. **1:1.** What is the importance here of the death of Joshua? What method do the people of Israel use to inquire of the Lord what to do? Where does Israel appear to be gathered?
3. **1:8.** What kind of place is Jerusalem at this point? Who overthrows the city and occupies it for a time? Who later will make it a permanent Israelite city?
4. **1:16.** Who is "the Kenite"? From where does the relationship between Israel and the Kenites stem? What did Moses promise certain Midianites, and in exchange for what? What do scholars infer from the Kenite name? What is the city of palms?
5. **1:23–26.** What does the takeover of Bethel recall? How are both stories similar? What is the critical difference between them?
6. **1:28.** What happens to Canaanites not destroyed or dislodged from the land? Of what does this give evidence, both positively and negatively?

For application
1. **1:1.** Whose death has meant the most to you on a personal level? Did it help to decide the direction of your life? If so, how?
2. **1:7.** Has something you did to others—be it a punishment you inflicted, an act of spite, or an impulsive deed that caused injury—ever been done to you in return? How serious was the matter? What did you learn from it about yourself or about God's justice?
3. **1:27-33.** What often happens to the culture of immigrants as they try to settle into a new country? What benefits does assimilation provide? What are some of its cultural drawbacks? What is likely to happen to the religious practices of immigrants who settle in places where there is disapproval of either their religion or its cultural expressions?

Chapter 2

For understanding
1. **2:1.** What is the "angel of the LORD", and how may he appear? How is the word *bochim* translated, and to what does it probably refer?
2. **2:11–3:6.** What does this theological preface to the stories in Judges 3–16 briefly outline? What is the twofold lesson? By what theological vision and vocabulary are these verses shaped?
3. **2:11.** Who is Baal? In Semitic mythology, what does he do? Why was Baal extremely important to the agricultural life of Canaan, and why is the name plural here?
4. **2:22.** What are the five reasons why the settlement of Canaan was a long and drawn-out process?

For application
1. **2:4.** Read the note for this verse. What is the difference between *remorse* and *repentance*? How should they be related? In the Passion narrative, which of Jesus' disciples showed remorse but did not repent, and which showed remorse along with repentance?
2. **2:10.** Because most children of Catholic parents are baptized as infants, what is the parents' responsibility in regard to their religious upbringing? Assuming the parents teach the faith to their children, what do the children need to do about it as they grow older? What does the expression "God has no grandchildren" mean?
3. **2:14.** What would likely happen to the faith of a Catholic who is irregular or neglectful in its practice if he lived in a culture that was openly unsupportive of his religion? How might such spiritual weakness be overcome?
4. **2:18-19.** It often happens that a person raised under the discipline of a strong tutor abandons that discipline when the tutor is no longer around. Is there anything in your experience that might illustrate this behavior pattern? In your judgment, what might account for it?

Chapter 3

For understanding
1. **3:3.** Where was Israel settled? Who are the Philistines, and from where do they come, according to the Bible? When do they establish themselves in southwest Canaan? Where are the Canaanites and the Sidonians located? Where are Baal-Hermon and Hamath?
2. **3:9.** Who is Othniel? What effort is he leading? Why is Othniel (along with Deborah) the most exemplary of the judges in the book?
3. **3:10.** What does the Spirit of the Lord bring to the judges? How does he accomplish this? What does the work of the Spirit in the lives of the judges anticipate?

4. **3:15.** Who is Ehud? How does he free Israel from 18 years of vassalage to the Moabites? In which tribe is being left-handed a common trait, and what is ironic about the name of this tribe? What form of tribute is Israel probably paying?
5. **3:31.** What is known about Shamgar? Since Anath is the name of a Semitic goddess of warfare, what do many surmise about Shamgar? What is an oxgoad? What story does Shamgar's success in wielding this unconventional weapon anticipate?

For application
1. **3:2.** Contrast this verse with Is 2:4; see also Eccles 3:8. When is it necessary to learn war, and when is it important to unlearn it? According to CCC 2307ff., what is the Catholic Church's teaching on the waging of war?
2. **3:4.** Why does God test people? How do you think that he sometimes tests you?
3. **3:6–7.** Why would mixed marriages such as these cause the people of Israel to do what is evil in the sight of the Lord? What dangers arise when people choose spouses who do not share their own religious commitments?
4. **3:8.** What is the "anger of the Lord"? Since Scripture elsewhere describes God as "jealous" (Ex 20:5; Deut 4:24), what is the relation of his "anger" to his infinite love? How does the image of God's anger affect your relationship with him?

Chapter 4

For understanding
1. **4:1—5:31.** Of what is the story of Deborah and Barak an account, in both prose and poetry? What do the heroic actions of Deborah and Jael in these episodes show about the role of women?
2. **4:4.** What does Deborah's name mean? What positions and kinds of influence does she hold? From which tribe does she hail? Alongside what other prominent figures of the Bible who perform judicial and prophetic functions does Deborah stand?
3. **4:6.** Who is Barak, and what does his name mean? For what is he later noted? Where are Kedesh and Mount Tabor?
4. **4:17.** What does Jael's name mean? From what ethnic group may she have come? What does the possibility that she might be an Israelite married into a Kenite family explain?

For application
1. **4:8.** Read the note for this verse. Since Barak's hesitation is a "momentary act of disobedience", why might he want Deborah to accompany him? Have you ever sought a similar kind of reassurance before starting a difficult project?
2. **4:9.** Barak's momentary disobedience has a personal consequence, since his success is not as great as it would have been if he had obeyed. Why does obedience require faith? If you distrust a command, how successful are you likely to be in carrying it out?
3. **4:15.** The note for this verse describes how the Lord intervenes to give Barak the victory despite what would ordinarily have been a tactical advantage for the enemy. Has the Lord ever intervened in your life to reverse a situation that appeared hopeless to you? If so, how did you thank him?

Chapter 5

For understanding
1. **5:1–31.** What does the Song of Deborah celebrate? Of what is it a classic specimen, and when was it possibly composed? Why are several lines hard to decipher?
2. **5:14–18.** As an assessment of the wartime response of Israel, which tribes are praised, and which are rebuked? Why are two tribes unmentioned? What does the poem make clear about Israel?
3. **5:20.** What do the stars represent? What does the next verse (5:21) suggest?
4. **5:31.** What does the prayer that Yahweh's friends would be like the sun mean? What does Scripture teach that the saints are destined to do?

For application
1. **5:1–3.** What are some reasons why people compose victory songs after a battle? How many such songs can you think of from the history of our country? How is addressing such a song to the Lord spiritually appropriate?
2. **5:9.** This verse praises the commanders of Israel who took command of a poorly equipped army (see v. 8 and its note). Under what circumstances have you been called on to exercise leadership? Going into the situation, how willing were you to lead? What kinds of strength did leadership call forth from you?
3. **5:20.** Read the note for this verse. How does the Church call on the help of angels to protect her from her enemies, particularly the evil one? Have you ever had occasion to call on your guardian angel for help?
4. **5:26–27.** What effect is the repetition in these verses intended to produce on the reader? How does it enhance appreciation of the Lord's victory in the overall contest?

Chapter 6

For understanding
1. **6:1—8:35.** Who is Gideon? What does his name mean? What question is central to this account, and what ideal does Gideon uphold? What do the people desire, however?
2. **6:11–24.** What do these verses recount? What five parallels with the call of Moses at the burning bush are noticeable?
3. **Word study: Trumpet (6:34).** What is a *shophar*? What are some of its uses, including the most frequent uses? As a liturgical instrument, what is its purpose? As a military instrument, how is it used? How might both aspects be combined?
4. **6:38.** Where was the technique of wringing dew out of fleece used? Allegorically, according to St. Ambrose, what does the dew on the fleece represent? Morally, why was the miracle performed on the threshing floor?

For application

1. **6:12.** How would you respond if an angel addressed you the same way he addressed Gideon? What sort of valor is required of Christians in this century?
2. **6:13.** Gideon's response to the angel is anything but faith-filled. Have the hardships in your life ever prompted a similar cynical response to the Lord?
3. **6:15–16.** Compare the Lord's reply to Gideon with his reply to St. Paul in 2 Cor 12:9. Has the Lord ever worked through your own weakness (e.g., an illness or a personal setback) to strengthen you or others with his grace?
4. **6:34.** Read the note for this verse. How does the Spirit "clothe" a person with himself? Some people are reluctant to allow the Holy Spirit to take possession of them; what do they fear? What changes are likely to occur in a person of whom the Spirit takes possession?
5. **6:36–40.** The expression "laying a fleece" has come to mean asking God for a sign indicating his approval of an intention or direction. When might "laying a fleece" be appropriate, and when might it indicate a lack of faith?

Chapter 7

For understanding

1. **7:2.** What was the purpose of Gideon's scaling back his army of 32,000 soldiers to a mere 300 men? What does Israel learn from this?
2. **7:6.** Why does Gideon select men for his army who lapped water from their hands rather than kneeling down to drink?
3. **7:10.** Who is Purah? How is the same Hebrew term rendered in 9:54 and in 1 Sam 14:1?
4. **7:19.** How was the night divided into watches? When did the middle watch begin?

For application

1. **7:2.** Has the Lord ever asked you to trust him rather than rely on your own resources? If so, did you try to bargain or compromise with him about that? When you get into an argument with the Lord, who wins?
2. **7:5.** How would you describe a position of spiritual alertness? For what, in our culture, should one be spiritually alert? What is the difference between a defensive posture of alertness and an offensive one? Which do you think is more necessary?
3. **7:10–11.** Sometimes, circumstances suggest a direction the Lord may wish you to take. How would you recognize such a direction? What role does regular (as opposed to occasional) prayer play in discerning his direction for you?
4. **7:15.** Think of an instance in your life when you knew the time for making up your mind was over and it was time to act. How did you recognize that point? On hindsight, how would you evaluate your decision?

Chapter 8

For understanding

1. **8:5.** Where is Succoth? With what modern site is it often identified? Why do city officials in Succoth refuse to supply Gideon's army with provisions? Who might the "kings of Midian" be?
2. **8:13–17.** What does Gideon do to Succoth and Penuel? Who sanctioned this action against Gideon's fellow Israelites? What does it anticipate?
3. **8:22–24.** What do the people want to do with Gideon? Why does he refuse the honor? What does the outcry for an earthly king (monarchy) show about Israel, and when will this be made clear?
4. **8:27.** To what does the term *ephod* typically refer? Why might Gideon have put forward the idea of using an ephod? What actually happens to it? What does collecting gold earrings for the making of a cult object recall about both Aaron and Moses? Despite doing the Lord's work and defending the Lord's honor, how does Gideon end up?

For application

1. **8:2–3.** Compare Gideon's reply to the Ephraimites with Prov 15:1. When faced with someone's anger, how do you typically tend to reply? After the confrontation has ended, how do you tend to judge your own part in it?
2. **8:5–9.** Gideon threatens (and later delivers) revenge on the Israelites who refuse to aid him. According to the Lord's Prayer, what should a Christian's response be? Assuming that someone in authority thinks punishment is necessary, what of a positive nature should it be designed to accomplish?
3. **8:20.** Have you ever been afraid to do what someone told you to? If so, what caused the fear? Has fear ever kept you from doing something you believed to be the Lord's desire for you?
4. **8:22–23.** Look up Deut 33:5, referred to in the note for these verses. What was the legal basis for keeping the Lord as the ruler of Israel? According to the Sermon on the Mount (Mt 5–7), on what basis should a Christian community govern its behavior?

Chapter 9

For understanding

1. **9:1–57.** What does this chapter recount? In what role is Abimelech cast? What characterizes his rule? What is the point of the story?
2. **9:1.** Where is Shechem? What is its connection with the Deuteronomic covenant under Joshua? What is happening there now, many years later? Who are Abimelech's kinsmen, and what assistance do they give him?
3. **9:7–15.** About what does Jotham's parable warn? What do the noble trees represent? How is Abimelech presented?
4. **9:23.** What does God's sending an evil spirit indicate? In this case, what is the demon given free rein to do? Theologically, what point is being made?

For application

1. **9:7–15.** Why would Jotham choose a parable as a way to deliver his message instead of simply stating his position in non-figurative language? What impact is a parable designed to have that is missing from a more direct approach?

Study Questions

2. **9:23.** The last sentence of the note for this verse raises a theological point about God's use of evildoing in the working out of his justice. Has an instance of wrongdoing, whether criminal or through negligence or some other cause, ever turned out for the good in your own or your family's experience? If so, what has that taught you about God's love or his mercy?

Chapter 10

For understanding
1. **10:1.** Who is Tola? What might his role as a deliverer and judge over Israel indicate? Where is Shamir?
2. **10:6—12:7.** Who is Jephthah? Though adept at diplomacy and military leadership, by what is his career overshadowed? From which tribe is he?
3. **10:6.** What does mention of the gods indicate? To which gods have the covenant people been attached, and which are they now worshiping?
4. **10:13.** For what does the Lord rebuke Israel? Though formally the statement sounds like a divine renunciation of the covenant, what is its aim?

For application
1. **10:6-7.** According to the chart *Victories of the Judges* (see notes for chap. 3), the judgeship of Tola and Jair resulted in 45 years of peace, after which Israel again abandoned the Lord. Why do peace and prosperity, when one is most free to practice his faith, often result in a relaxation of religious observance (see Deut 8:11-20)? How do persecution and oppression work to bring about a return to the Lord?
2. **10:10-16.** According to the same *Victories of the Judges* chart, the next period of oppression and prayer for help lasted 18 years. What shape did the people's repentance take? How long might a national process of putting "away the foreign gods" have taken? What would have been involved? Why do repentance and conversion take so long?
3. **10:16.** The note for this verse discusses what "he became indignant" might mean. As a parent, how would you respond to a child who repeatedly gets into trouble despite your warnings and who always expects you to help? What limits might there be to God's patience?

Chapter 11

For understanding
1. **11:15-27.** With what do these verses deal? What arguments does Jephthah use to contest the claim that Israel illegally occupies the lands east of the Jordan?
2. **11:24.** Who is Chemosh? Why might Jephthah make reference to Chemosh instead of the Moabite national god Molech? Who gave the Ammonites their land, according to the Torah?
3. **11:29-40.** What did Jephthah inadvertently but recklessly promise? What did the resulting predicament mean for his daughter and for his family? What are two different ways that commentators have understood the nature of Jephthah's sacrifice? Explain how these different interpretations lead to different assessments of the character of Jephthah.
4. **11:34.** How were victory celebrations traditionally led? The same Hebrew expression for an "only child" is used for what other biblical character? How are the two events, while similar, mirror opposites?
5. **11:37.** Why does Jephthah's daughter lament her virginity? Why was this a painful burden? How did the attitude toward sexual abstinence gradually change?

For application
1. **11:3.** In today's urban environments, what often happens to young men with leadership skills who have nothing to do but roam the streets? What fate often awaits them as a result? Have you heard (or experienced) stories where such young people have been turned into responsible citizens? What role, if any, have you played in this process?
2. **11:30-31.** St. Ignatius of Loyola's *Rules for the Discernment of Spirits* advise against making vows to the Lord under the influence of spiritual euphoria. If you have ever made a rash promise to the Lord, what was the nature of it? What efforts did you make to fulfill it, and what was the outcome? What did you learn from the experience?
3. **11:37.** What is the attitude toward virginity in our culture? What respect have you had toward this virtue? How does the reason for Jephthah's daughter's lament for her virginity challenge our culture's attitudes toward children?

Chapter 12

For understanding
1. **12:1-6.** What happens in these verses? Between whom is the clash? Why are the Ephraimites offended? How does Jephthah respond? What does it seem that Ephraim, one of the largest and strongest of the twelve tribes, is challenging?
2. **12:6.** What does the word *shibboleth* mean? How are fleeing Ephraimites exposed at the Jordan River checkpoint?
3. **12:8.** Who is Ibzan? To which Bethlehem is this probably a reference?
4. **12:13.** Who is Abdon? What do we know about his hometown and the man himself?

For application
1. **12:1-3.** Have quarrels, misunderstandings, or grievances (real or imagined) ever affected relationships in your extended family? If so, how have family members tried to restore peace? Whose responsibility is it to forgive offenses?
2. **12:6.** In this verse, the Gileadites use a password to identify an enemy trying to sneak past them. According to Mt 7:21, how will the Son of Man recognize those who try to gain entrance into heaven?
3. **12:9.** Given the tensions in Israel, what might Ibzan have sought to gain by arranging marriages outside his clan? What is marriage supposed to accomplish between husband and wife? How might the marriage bond help strengthen relationships within an extended family?

Chapter 13

For understanding
1. **13:1–16:31.** With what do these chapters deal? What impels Samson, more than his predecessors, to accomplish his mission? What factors make Samson a tragic figure? How does he overcome his many failings in the end? What is one of the many lessons conveyed by his story?
2. **13:4.** Why did the angel of the Lord warn Manoah's wife to eat nothing unclean?
3. **13:5.** What is a Nazirite? From what did Nazirites vow to abstain? How was the vow normally taken, and for how long? Why was Samson unusual in his consecration, and how committed was he to it? How does Samson prefigure John the Baptist? At what does the expression "begin to deliver" hint?
4. **13:24.** To what Hebrew word is Samson's name related? How will the importance of this be revealed later?

For application
1. **13:3–5.** Compare the angel's announcement of Samson's birth to Gabriel's announcement to Zechariah of John the Baptist's birth (Lk 1:13–17). What are the main similarities? What are the main differences? What does the angel say about the role of each child?
2. **13:8.** Compare Manoah's prayer in this verse with his question to the angel in v. 12. For what is the prospective father really asking? If you have children, what do you pray for regarding them?
3. **13:12-14.** What do you think of the angel's answer to Manoah's question? Why does he seem to insist on the *mother's* holiness rather than her son's (review also vv. 4–5 above)?
4. **13:25.** When the Spirit of the Lord "stirs" someone, what is likely to be the result? According to 2 Tim 1:6, what characteristics does the Spirit impart to us? Of these characteristics, which seems to be prominent in the story of Samson?

Chapter 14

For understanding
1. **14:3.** Why do Samson's parents have strong reservations about a mixed marriage? What was the danger? What kinds of marriage were encouraged in Israel? What does the appearance of Samson's idiom "she is right in my eyes" anticipate?
2. **14:9.** Why does Samson not reveal to his parents that he has taken honey from the carcass of the lion and that he has touched the carcass? Allegorically, according to St. Ambrose, what is the lion, and what kind of honey comes from its body?
3. **14:10.** What does the Hebrew word *mishteh* mean specifically? What does it imply that Samson did? What kind of celebration is this?
4. **14:20.** What role does Samson's best man have? In later Judaism, what was the best man at a wedding called?

For application
1. **14:3.** Why has the Catholic Church traditionally urged her members to choose spouses who are Catholic? Although mixed marriages are common in our culture, what difficulties do spouses from different Christian traditions typically face in such marriages? What difficulties might occur if one of the spouses is unbaptized?
2. **14:4.** Read the notes for vv. 9 and 10. What authority over himself does Samson appear to recognize? What authority over their own behavior do many young people recognize today? How does acceptance of a moral law result in personal freedom, and how does abandonment of such a law restrict or eliminate it?
3. **14:16-17.** Samson's bride pressures her husband through tears and accusations to tell her what she wants to know. How do you usually try to get your way with a spouse, parent, or other authority figure? How have others tried to get their way with you? Assuming the tactics worked, what have been the long-term effects for the relationships involved?

Chapter 15

For understanding
1. **15:1.** When is the wheat harvest? Where does Samson's bride continue to live? Why does Samson bring a kid to her? What is his intent?
2. **15:2.** What does Samson's father-in-law think has happened to his newly married daughter that makes her in need of a new husband? To what might the word "hate" also refer, and how was it used in Jewish divorce certificates?
3. **15:11.** What was the Judahite's willingness to surrender Samson to the Philistines an attempt to avoid?
4. **15:18.** How many times in Judges does Samson become moved to prayer? How does God respond?

For application
1. **15:3.** Samson regards himself as blameless in taking revenge on the Philistines. Do you have any experience with revenge? If so, what excuses were given for seeking it? Why does Scripture say that revenge belongs to the Lord? Since the Lord is a God of mercy and compassion, of what is his revenge likely to consist?
2. **15:8-9.** How do acts of revenge tend to escalate? In Mt 5:9, why does Jesus say that peacemakers will be sons of God? In what ways are they like him?
3. **15:18.** What is the tone of Samson's prayer? How do you approach God when you are in desperate need of something? How do you approach him when you have no need of anything?

Chapter 16

For understanding
1. **16:20.** Where does Samson's physical strength actually reside? Why is shaving off Samson's hair so important in terms of his consecration? Morally, according to St. Paulinus of Nola, how is the spiritual plight of sinners compared to the bodily suffering of Samson?

2. **16:23.** Who is Dagon, and for what is he revered? Why is Dagon praised for the capture of Samson? Ironically, what divinity arranges Samson's apprehension?
3. **16:28.** In weakness, what has Samson come to realize? For what is Samson remembered in the New Testament?
4. **16:30.** How many Philistines does Samson fell in this crowning moment? Allegorically, according to St. Paulinus of Nola, what does the death of Samson prefigure? According to St. Caesarius of Arles, what does the fact that more perished at his death than in his life signify about Christ, the true Samson?

For application
1. **16:6–17.** What is it that so captivates us about other people's secrets? What do we expect to gain by learning them? What harm do we do ourselves through undue curiosity?
2. **16:20.** What gives you your spiritual strength? What would cause the Lord to withdraw his grace or his help in time of need? How would you regain the strength you lost?
3. **16:28.** According to the note for this verse, Samson acknowledges his total dependence on God. Why is such an acknowledgment important for one's spiritual life? Just as Samson's use of his free will gets him into such trouble, how does the surrender of free will to God result in spiritual benefit?
4. **16:30.** Do you interpret Samson's life and its outcome as a success or a failure? Why? What makes one's life a success or a failure, especially in the eyes of God? In which direction do you see your own life going?

Chapter 17

For understanding
1. **17:1—21:25.** As what does this epilogue to Judges serve? If earlier chapters underscored the threat that foreign aggressors posed to Israel, what do these final chapters show? Of what two accounts does the epilogue consist? Around what are these final chapters held together?
2. **17:3.** Though Micah's mother shows commendable devotion to Yahweh, how does she appear to be ignorant of the Torah? Of what is her religion a mixture?
3. **17:5.** While an ephod normally refers to a decorated vestment worn by the high priest of Israel, to what may the reference be here? What are *teraphim*? What made Micah's son ineligible to be installed as a priest?
4. **17:10.** Of what is priesthood a cultic expression? How does this idea have a basis in biblical history? How does the New Testament bear witness to it? What belief has the Church asserted as recently as Vatican II?

For application
1. **17:3.** What does the *Catechism* have to say about superstition (CCC 2110–11, 2138)? Has superstition of any sort affected your faith life? If you have engaged in any sort of superstitious practices, what caused you to turn away from them?
2. **17:5.** Do you have a kind of "sacred space" in your home, such as a shrine to Mary or another one of the saints? What does it contain? What use do you make of it?
3. **17:6.** The note for this verse points to the text as a refrain in Judges. What is the problem with doing what is right in one's own eyes? What role is conscience supposed to play in one's behavior?
4. **17:10.** Read the note for this verse. How do you regard the role of a priest? Is calling him "Father" merely a title or something more? If the latter, how does your regard show itself in the ways you speak about priests to other Catholics or non-Catholics?

Chapter 18

For understanding
1. **18:1–31.** What story does Judges 18 recount? What territory was originally allotted to Dan, and why were the Danites unable to secure it? After spying out the land, what do the Danites opt to do? What does the text of Judges say about God's approval or the motive for the Danites' undertaking?
2. **18:7.** Archaeologically, where is Laish situated? To what does archaeological evidence point in terms of a date for the Danite conquest? How do the Danite spies describe the town? Since Laish has formed no alliances with other city-states, what is its military situation?
3. **18:14–20.** What do the 600 armed Danites do to Micah? How is their thievery an instance of poetic justice?
4. **18:30.** Of what is Dan made the center? What does transfer of the idol and priest from Ephraim to Dan anticipate? Who is Jonathan, and what is his relationship to Moses? How does Judges draw a sharp contrast between Jonathan and Phinehas? Why, according to some scholars, does the Hebrew text substitute the name "Manasseh" for that of Moses? To what does the chronological note "until the day of the captivity" refer?

For application
1. **18:18–20.** What would you say of the loyalty of an employee who was trained for service in one company but, on completing the training, left for employment at a competitor whose wages were greater?
2. **18:24.** If you have had property stolen from you, what primarily concerned you about the theft? How did it affect you personally?
3. **18:30.** Read what the *Catechism* says about graven images (CCC 2129–32 and cross references). How do Catholics justify the veneration of icons of Christ and the saints?

Chapter 19

For understanding
1. **19:1.** Who is the Levite in this verse? What is a concubine? Where is the Bethlehem mentioned in the verse?
2. **19:22–26.** What does Gibeah do to its guests? What do the multiple parallels between the men of Gibeah and the men of Sodom indicate?

3. **Word Study: Know (19:22).** What does the Hebrew verb *yada'* mean? In Hebrew thinking, how does a person come to possess knowledge? What does it mean to know intellectually? experientially? by revelation? In several passages, for what is the verb a euphemism? How is knowing in this sense gravely sinful?
4. **19:29.** As what does the Levite's ghastly deed function? What was it meant to do?

For application
1. **19:4-9.** What are some of the cultural stereotypes we have of family in-laws? How well do you know your own in-laws or any of the in-laws associated with your family? How would you characterize your relationships with them?
2. **19:15-21.** If you were traveling to an unfamiliar city, would you choose to stay at a hotel, the home of a relative or family friend, or with a member of the local Catholic community? If the last is not on your list of choices, why not? If you knew that a welcoming Catholic community was available for you, what difference would that make?
3. **19:24-26.** How do you react to this story of rape? Why do you think the inspired author included it? What does the *Catechism* (CCC 2356, 2389) have to say about crimes of this sort?
4. **19:29-30.** Read CCC 364 and 2300. What kind of respect do we owe to the bodies of the deceased? Why, according to the Order of Christian Funerals (§417), is the practice of scattering the ashes of cremated remains or keeping them in a private home forbidden?

Chapter 20

For understanding
1. **20:1.** What does the stock expression "Dan to Beersheba" mean? Where is Gilead? What sense about Israel remains despite the intertribal tensions and conflicts throughout the period of the Judges? Where is Mizpah?
2. **20:18.** Where is Bethel, and to what is it host? Most likely, from what sanctuary was the Ark transferred and where was it later returned? How was inquiry made of the Lord? Why is the selection of Judah to lead the attack a logical choice?
3. **20:28.** Who is Phinehas? What is his position in Israel, in contrast to the illegitimate priest Jonathan? What does Phinehas' appearance in this account indicate about the civil war against Benjamin?
4. **20:35.** What is the idea behind Benjamin's defeat, predicted by the oracle? In what guise is Yahweh often depicted, and what is different about this case?

For application
1. **20:12-13.** The *Catechism* lists *fraternal correction* as one of the fruits of charity, or love (CCC 1829), and as one of the forms that conversion takes (CCC 1435). Have you ever been corrected for your conduct by a sibling or a religious peer? If so, did you accept it as an act of love and a call to conversion? The *Catechism* (2540) links humility with the sin of envy; why is that?
2. **20:25.** Read the note for this verse, particularly the last sentence. Why is sin not a private matter? How does your sin bring suffering on others? In that light, then, what virtue should prompt you to go to confession and make reparation?
3. **20:28.** After two failed efforts, taken at the Lord's direction, the Israelites ask the Lord whether a third effort is worth making. Have you ever been tempted to give up after repeated failures, even though you thought you were doing the Lord's will? If so, how did you learn that the Lord wanted you to continue trying?

Chapter 21

For understanding
1. **21:1-24.** To what dilemma did the massacre of the Benjaminites give rise? What oath complicated the crisis? To what strange but creative solution did the assembly resort? What was the Lord's involvement in either tactic?
2. **21:8.** What loophole does the settlement of Jabesh-gilead represent in the sworn pledges made at Mizpah?
3. **21:19.** What feast of the Lord is celebrated here? How do some commentators envision it? What is significant about its occurrence at Shiloh?
4. **21:25.** What is the threefold historical, canonical, and political significance of the refrain that "in those days there was no king in Israel"? What is doing "what was right in his own eyes" a way of saying? From where does the expression come? How will David rise above the chaos of the times?

For application
1. **21:7.** CCC 2150-55 covers the topic of oaths. Why could the Israelites not have simply dispensed themselves from fulfilling the oaths they took to deny the surviving Benjaminites their daughters in marriage (cf. v. 18)? How serious is the obligation to keep an oath? If you have ever taken a civil or religious oath, how seriously did you regard keeping it?
2. **21:14.** From this verse and the remainder of the chapter, what might you infer was the main purpose of marriage in Israel? How different is that purpose from the purposes of marriage in our culture? Why do you think contraception has taken such a hold in our culture?
3. **21:16-24.** Read the note for these verses. What is the difference between a *reason* for an action and a *rationalization* for it? For what kinds of behavior do people tend to rationalize? What does rationalization do to a person's character?
4. **21:25.** Why is doing what is right in one's own eyes not necessarily a good thing? Why is the formation of conscience important? According to what standard should one's conscience be formed?

INTRODUCTION TO RUTH

Author and Date The origins of the Book of Ruth are obscure. Neither the identity of the author nor the time of the book's composition is known with certainty. Jewish rabbinic tradition ascribes the work to the prophet Samuel (Babylonian Talmud, *Baba Bathra* 14b). More recently, some have suggested that the prophet Nathan, a member of David's royal court, may have been its author, while others, taking note of the narrator's sensitive depiction of female concerns and relationships, have argued that the writer is a woman. None of these proposals is strictly impossible, but neither is any likely to be proven. All are examples of educated guesswork. For this reason, a majority of scholars are content to say that the author remains unknown.

Efforts to date the Book of Ruth have generated a broad range of opinions. Most can be plotted on a spectrum between the tenth century and the fifth century B.C. Some scholars, reading the book as a *promotional* tract designed to enhance or defend the reputation of King David, prefer to date its composition during the years of his reign, between ca. 1010 and 970 B.C. Other scholars, reading the book as a *polemical* tract that implicitly criticizes the policies of Ezra and Nehemiah against mixed marriages, assign it a date in the mid-400s B.C., when intermarriage with foreigners was a burning social and religious issue in Israel. Still other commentators have argued for various dates and circumstances between these outer limits. Linguistic analysis, far from settling the issue, has yielded results that could be used to support any viable position. On the one hand, much of the story is written in the classical Hebrew that was used in the preexilic period (before 586 B.C.); on the other hand, signs of late biblical Hebrew and of Aramaic influence have also been pointed out and taken as evidence of a postexilic date (after 538 B.C.).

The evidence is perhaps best accommodated by distinguishing a first edition of the book from its final edition. Several indicators, for instance, suggest an original composition in the historical setting of David's kingship: David is named twice in the book, even though the story takes place well before his lifetime (4:17, 22); the principal setting for the account is David's hometown of Bethlehem (1:22); and the genealogy that ends the book extends from patriarchal times down to David, with no mention of his descendants or successors (4:18–22). Even so, grammatical features distinctive of the postexilic period are in evidence as well.

One plausible scenario would allow that the Book of Ruth first appeared in the tenth century B.C., during the time of David, but that some of its wording was updated by a scribe editing the book in the postexilic period.

Title The Hebrew title of the book is *Ruth*, the name of the Moabite maiden who features as one of the pivotal figures of the story. Her name may be a play on the Hebrew word *re'uth*, meaning "friendship". Ruth is the only book of the OT named after a Gentile and is one of only three books of the Bible named after a woman, alongside Esther and Judith. The Greek Septuagint (LXX) transliterates the title as *Routh*, and the Latin Vulgate supplies the fuller heading *Liber Ruth*, "Book of Ruth".

Structure The book may be outlined according to its settings. Four localities provide the backdrop for most of the action and dialogue. **(1)** The story begins in *Moab*, where Ruth determines to follow the grieving Naomi back to Israel (1:1). **(2)** Thereafter developments take place at a *field* in Bethlehem where Ruth encounters Boaz (2:2). **(3)** Ruth then takes proactive steps at a *threshing floor* in Bethlehem to make known to Boaz her eligibility for marriage (3:2). **(4)** Finally, the opportunity arrives at the city *gate* in Bethlehem for Boaz to claim the right of redemption and to marry the widowed Ruth (4:1). The closing genealogy serves as a short but significant appendix (4:18–22). See *Outline*.

Place in the Canon Christian editions of the Bible follow the Greek Septuagint and Latin Vulgate in placing the Book of Ruth among the Historical Books between Judges and First Samuel. This arrangement takes its cue from the opening verse, which situates the story during "the days when the judges ruled" (1:1). In the Hebrew canon, Ruth is placed in the third division of the Old Testament, called the Writings, among a group of five scrolls that were read on major Jewish feast days. Ruth was traditionally read at the annual Feast of Weeks, also known as Pentecost, in late spring. So far as evidence indicates, there were no significant objections to the canonical status of Ruth in either Jewish or Christian antiquity.

Literary Genre Scholars debate whether the Book of Ruth is fictional or historical. It is by all accounts a masterpiece of ancient storytelling. But is the storyline a product of memory or imagination? Some classify the work as a folktale, novella, or idyll—the latter being a genre that romanticizes the simplicity of pastoral life. From this perspective, one can speak of the lessons and aims of the book, but not of actual events and occurrences underlying the narrative. Others, to the contrary, classify the work as an edifying short story about the real experiences of real people. On this view, Ruth is an abbreviated account of family history, albeit one told with literary elegance and charm.

Without denying or downplaying the artistic skills of the author, there are several reasons for considering the Book of Ruth a historical short story. Besides the fact that it portrays accurately the conditions of life in a rural community in biblical times, the story is situated in a known historical period (time of the judges, 1:1), unfolds in known historical places (Moab, Bethlehem), and makes reference to known historical persons (Jesse, David). Its historiographical intent is also suggested by the concluding genealogy, which anchors the account in Israel's sacred history. Indeed, the same pre-Davidic bloodline that appears in 4:18–22 is presented elsewhere in the Bible as authentic archival information (1 Chron 2:5–15). Finally, it is highly improbable that a writer of fiction would make David's great-grandmother Ruth a Moabite rather than a faithful Israelite, especially since David himself conquered the Moabites and made them vassals subject to Israel (2 Sam 8:2).

Themes and Characteristics The Book of Ruth is a small but dazzling gem of the Old Testament. It is a beam of light piercing the moral and spiritual gloom that shrouds the period of the judges. Practically all the characters of the book are admirable to one degree or another, and none can be called a villain or antagonist. Despite the general corruption of the times, it reveals that certain families in Israel remained faithful to the Lord and loyal to one another, especially among the common folk.

The Book of Ruth revolves around family life and family obligations. The storyline may be said to swing upward from bereavement to blessing, from the death of several loved ones to the joyous birth of a new generation. Tragedy strikes at the outset, when the Israelite matriarch Naomi loses her husband and two sons during their temporary sojourn in Moab (1:1–5). Grief and widowhood then force Naomi and her Moabite daughters-in-law, Orpah and Ruth, to make important decisions about their future. For Naomi and Ruth, this means traveling back to Bethlehem and living among the kinsfolk of Naomi's deceased husband, Elimelech (1:6–22). From this point on things get steadily better. Ruth, though a Moabite rather than an Israelite, is singled out and favored by an upstanding relative of Elimelech named Boaz (2:1–23). One thing leads to another, and on the advice of Naomi, Ruth reveals her family connection to Boaz with

the hope that marriage might eventuate (3:1–18). Boaz, a near kinsman, is eligible to claim the right of redemption in caring for the widows and fathering an heir for the late Elimelech. Already attentive to Ruth and her needs, he wastes no time in taking the necessary steps to acquire Naomi's estate and secure the hand of Ruth in marriage (4:1–12). To the delight of all, the union is fruitful, and Ruth mothers a son, Obed, who is destined to continue the family line and restore to Naomi the happiness that seemed forever lost (4:13–17).

More than just a heartwarming tale at the human level, the Book of Ruth has subtle but significant things to say about the mystery of divine Providence. Throughout the whole movement from suffering to celebration, the reader is invited to ponder the Lord's role in the story. God never thunders from heaven or bursts on the scene with mighty miracles or stunning revelations, yet there is a sense that even the most ordinary events are guided by his hidden hand. At several critical steps, readers witness divine "coincidences" in which the Lord steers the actions of this family and blesses them in ways that have an impact, not only on the lives of the individuals involved, but also on the unfolding of salvation history in general. Boaz in particular embodies the loving kindness of God toward Naomi and Ruth. His willingness to play the part of the kinsman redeemer, to rescue these women from the burdens of a bleak and joyless future, is a tangible of sign of the Lord's care for his faithful ones.

Among other aims, it is likely that Ruth was written to explain how God preserved the royal line of Judah at a time of crisis. It is a pivotal chapter in the backstory leading up to David and the founding of the Israelite monarchy. Had the Lord not intervened in the life of Naomi and her family, her deceased husband's line would have been extinguished and Israel's most admired king, David, the son of Jesse, would never have been born. At the same time, the book helps to explain how David, a man of remarkable faith and spiritual vision, could emerge from such a dark period of history. Detailing the actions and motives of David's virtuous ancestors indicates that he hailed from a family of unusual devotion and noble character.

Christian Perspective The significance of the Book of Ruth is apparent from the opening lines of the New Testament, where we learn that Boaz and Ruth are not only ancestors of the memorable King David but distant relatives of his messianic descendant, Jesus Christ (Mt 1:1–16). Beyond this, Christian faith sees in Ruth an example of Gentile conversion. She, though a Moabite, made a conscious decision to leave behind her people and her gods and find refuge under the wings of the God of Israel (2:11–12). Her willingness to abandon the past and adopt the ways of the covenant people is summed up in her pledge of loyalty to Naomi: "Entreat me not to leave you or to return from following you; for where you go I will go, and where you lodge I will lodge; your people shall be my people, and your God my God" (1:16). In this respect Ruth anticipates the faith of Gentiles who will flock to the one true God in messianic times (cf. 1 Thess 1:9).

OUTLINE OF RUTH

1. From Moab to Bethlehem (1:1–22)
   A. Widowed in Moab (1:1–5)
   B. Ruth Clings to Naomi and to the Lord (1:6–22)

2. At a Field in Bethlehem (2:1–23)
   A. Ruth Wins the Favor of Boaz (2:1–16)
   B. Ruth Informs Naomi (2:17–23)

3. At a Threshing Floor in Bethlehem (3:1–18)
   A. Ruth Approaches Boaz (3:1–13)
   B. Ruth Informs Naomi (3:14–18)

4. At the Gate of Bethlehem (4:1–22)
   A. Boaz Finds Next-of-Kin (4:1–6)
   B. Boaz Claims and Marries Ruth (4:7–17)
   C. The Ancestry of David (4:18–22)

THE BOOK OF

RUTH

Elimelech's Family Goes to Moab

1 In the days when the judges ruled there was a famine in the land, and a certain man of Bethlehem in Judah went to sojourn in the country of Moab, he and his wife and his two sons. ²The name of the man was Elim'elech and the name of his wife Na'omi, and the names of his two sons were Mahlon and Chil'ion; they were Eph'rathites from Bethlehem in Judah. They went into the country of Moab and remained there. ³But Elim'elech, the husband of Na'omi, died, and she was left with her two sons. ⁴These took Moabite wives; the name of the one was Orpah and the name of the other Ruth. They lived there about ten years; ⁵and both Mahlon and Chil'ion died, so that the woman was bereft of her two sons and her husband.

Naomi and Her Moabite Daughters-in-law

6 Then she started with her daughters-in-law to return from the country of Moab, for she had heard in the country of Moab that the Lord had visited his people and given them food. ⁷So she set out from the place where she was, with her two daughters-in-law, and they went on the way to return to the land of Judah. ⁸But Na'omi said to her two daughters-in-law, "Go, return each of you to her mother's house. May the Lord deal kindly with you, as you have dealt with the dead and with me. ⁹The Lord grant that you may find a home, each of you in the house of her husband!" Then she kissed them, and they lifted up their voices and wept. ¹⁰And they said to her, "No, we will return with you to your people." ¹¹But Na'omi said, "Turn back, my daughters, why will you go with me? Have I yet sons in my womb that they may become your husbands? ¹²Turn back, my daughters, go your way, for I am too old to have a husband. If I should say I have hope, even if I should have a husband this night and should bear sons, ¹³would you therefore wait till they were grown? Would you therefore refrain from marrying? No, my daughters, for it is exceedingly bitter to me for your sake that the hand of the Lord has gone forth against me." ¹⁴Then they lifted up their voices and wept again; and Orpah kissed her mother-in-law, but Ruth clung to her.

1:1 the judges: Tribal leaders and warriors who settled disputes and delivered Israel from oppression in the centuries before the founding of the Davidic monarchy (Judg 2:16). The story of Ruth is set near the end of this period, around 1100 B.C. The loyalty displayed by its main characters contrasts sharply with the lawlessness that otherwise prevailed during the chaotic period of the judges (Judg 21:25). **Bethlehem:** Five miles south of Jerusalem. It is the hometown of the future King David (1 Sam 16:1) and the topographical setting for most of the book (1:19). Ironically, the story begins with a food shortage in Bethlehem, which means "house of bread". **sojourn:** For similar accounts of famine leading God's people to find refuge in a foreign land, see Gen 12:10 and 26:1. **Moab:** Southeast of the Dead Sea. The Moabites were longstanding enemies of Israel (Num 22:3–6; Judg 3:12–14). Intermarriage with them was not strictly prohibited, but Moabites were forbidden to join the worshiping assembly of Israel (Deut 23:3). Scripture traces the origin of the Moabites to the incestuous union between Lot and his daughter (Gen 19:30–37).

1:2 Elimelech: Ruth's father-in-law. His name in Hebrew means "my God is king." **Naomi:** Ruth's mother-in-law. Her name means "pleasant". **Ephrathites:** Ephrathah was a clan of the tribe of Judah settled in the Bethlehem area (Mic 5:2).

1:4 Orpah: Ruth's sister-in-law. Her name may mean "back of the neck", hinting at how she will turn away from Naomi and return to her people (1:15). **Ruth:** Her name resembles the Hebrew word for "friendship" and so bespeaks her most admirable virtue (1:17). Another possible meaning is "refreshment".

1:5 Mahlon: Ruth's husband (4:10). **Chilion:** Orpah's husband. **the woman was bereft:** All three men in Naomi's family fled hunger in Israel only to find death in Moab. The main crisis of the story is thus introduced: Elimelech's family line appears destined to die out. From the perspective of the author, who is writing at a later time, the royal line of David hangs in the balance awaiting God's intervention (4:18–22).

1:6 the Lord had visited: The first of several times in Ruth that the narrator perceives the hand of God's Providence working behind the scenes of the story (1:13, 21; 2:20; 4:13–14) (CCC 302–3).

1:7 land of Judah: The highlands west of the Dead Sea (Josh 15:1–63).

1:8 kindly: The Hebrew ḥesed denotes "faithful devotion" or "family loyalty". Because Ruth has shown kindness to Naomi and continues to show resolute commitment to her family (3:10), the Lord will manifest his loving concern for Ruth by arranging her marriage with Boaz (2:20; 4:13). The lesson, in part, is that God blesses those who bless the descendants of Abraham (Gen 12:3). For more on ḥesed, see word study: *Merciful Love* at Ex 34:7.

1:9 house of her husband: Naomi advises the young widows to remarry. In this way they can reclaim a measure of economic security and personal happiness.

1:11 Have I yet sons: The impossible desire to give Orpah and Ruth other sons suggests Naomi is thinking of the levirate law of Deuteronomy, which obliges an eligible brother to marry the widow of his deceased brother in the event that the first marriage produced no children (Deut 25:5–6).

This charming tale of family life in the countryside of Bethlehem during the period of the judges is imbued with a deeply religious spirit. It is a story of family devotion and of piety toward one's ancestors. The book has significance for the ancestry of David and the Messiah. Though Jewish in feeling, it is not narrowly so; indeed, Boaz goes beyond what is strictly required by the law and, though the book insists that Israel's faith must remain uncontaminated, yet it also says it must be made available to all. The call of the Gentiles is foreseen. There is no certainty about the date of the book. It was probably written during the period of the kingship, though some think it was composed after the Exile.

15 And she said, "See, your sister-in-law has gone back to her people and to her gods; return after your sister-in-law." ¹⁶But Ruth said, "Entreat me not to leave you or to return from following you; for where you go I will go, and where you lodge I will lodge; your people shall be my people, and your God my God; ¹⁷where you die I will die, and there will I be buried. May the Lord do so to me and more also if even death parts me from you." ¹⁸And when Na'omi saw that she was determined to go with her, she said no more.

19 So the two of them went on until they came to Bethlehem. And when they came to Bethlehem, the whole town was stirred because of them; and the women said, "Is this Na'omi?" ²⁰She said to them, "Do not call me Na'omi,ᵃ call me Mara,ᵇ for the Almighty has dealt very bitterly with me. ²¹I went away full, and the Lord has brought me back empty. Why call me Na'omi, when the Lord has afflictedᶜ me and the Almighty has brought calamity upon me?"

22 So Na'omi returned, and Ruth the Moabitess her daughter-in-law with her, who returned from the country of Moab. And they came to Bethlehem at the beginning of barley harvest.

Ruth Meets Boaz

2 Now Na'omi had a kinsman of her husband's, a man of wealth, of the family of Elim'elech, whose name was Boaz. ²And Ruth the Moabitess said to Na'omi, "Let me go to the field, and glean among the ears of grain after him in whose sight I shall find favor." And she said to her, "Go, my daughter." ³So she set forth and went and gleaned in the field after the reapers; and she happened to come to the part of the field belonging to Boaz, who was of the family of Elim'elech. ⁴And behold, Boaz came from Bethlehem; and he said to the reapers, "The Lord be with you!" And they answered, "The Lord bless you." ⁵Then Boaz said to his servant who was in charge of the reapers, "Whose maiden is this?" ⁶And the servant who was in charge of the reapers answered, "It is the Moabite maiden, who came back with Na'omi from the country of Moab. ⁷She said, 'Please, let me glean and gather among the sheaves after the reapers.' So she came, and

---

1:15 her gods: The deities revered by the Moabites, most notably the god Chemosh (Num 21:29). It was common in biblical antiquity for Gentile peoples to invoke the patronage of one or more national deities.

1:16–17 Ruth pledges lifelong loyalty to Naomi and solemnizes the commitment with an oath in the name of Yahweh. In so doing, she not only becomes the legal equivalent of Naomi's kinswoman, destined to be buried in the same family tomb, but she unites herself to the people of Israel (**my people**) and transfers her allegiance to the God of Israel (**my God**). Forsaking her home and native religion, Ruth voluntarily embraces a new way of life in the Lord's covenant community and thus serves as a model of Gentile conversion (2:11–12) (CCC 160, 2010). • *Morally*, when the sisters part, with Ruth following her mother-in-law and Orpah forsaking her, the one models fidelity, and the other infidelity. The one puts God ahead of homeland, the other, homeland ahead of life. Such discord extends through the cosmos, with some following God and others the world (St. Paulinus of Nola, *Poems* 27).

1:17 the Lord do so to me: An abbreviated curse formula. Ruth is invoking the judgment of God upon herself should she betray her pledge to Naomi in the future. The nature of the curse is not specified in the words of the oath but may have been acted out with a symbolic gesture. This idiom appears often in the OT (e.g., 2 Sam 3:35; 1 Kings 2:23; 2 Kings 6:31).

1:18 she said no more: Indicates resignation and acceptance rather than frustration.

1:20 the Almighty: The Hebrew epithet is *shadday*, the meaning of which is uncertain. A popular suggestion is the translation: "the One of the mountain".

1:21 full: Blessed with a family. **empty:** Bereaved of a husband and two sons.

1:22 barley harvest: In late spring. Famine giving way to a fruitful harvest anticipates how the lives of Ruth and Naomi are about to emerge from hardship (widowhood, 1:3–5) into newfound happiness (motherhood and grand-motherhood, 4:13–17).

2:1 Boaz: The third main character in the book after Ruth and Naomi. He is a close relative of Ruth's deceased father-in-law, Elimelech, and a man of significant wealth and standing in Bethlehem. The meaning of the name Boaz is uncertain but possibly "in him is strength."

2:2 the Moabitess: The foreign ancestry of Ruth is stressed throughout the chapter (see 2:6, 10, 21). **glean:** I.e., gather up the ears of barley dropped or otherwise left behind after the reapers have harvested the field. The Torah required landowners to leave a small portion of their crop unharvested as a charity offering for the poor (Lev 19:9–10). Impoverished widows like Ruth and Naomi had little choice but to scrounge for food in such ways in order to survive.

2:3 happened to come: The narrator describes as happenstance what the reader is meant to interpret as divine Providence. See note on 1:6.

2:4 the Lord be with you: Shows Boaz to be a religious man whose devotion to Yahweh carries over into his relationships in the workplace.

2:7 Please, let me: Shows Ruth to be gentle and polite. **without resting:** Shows Ruth to be hardworking and dedicated to supporting the elderly Naomi.

ᵃ That is *Pleasant*.
ᵇ That is *Bitter*.
ᶜ Gk Syr Vg: Heb *testified against*.

WORD STUDY

Clung (1:14)

Dabaq (Heb.): a verb meaning to "cleave", "cling", or "hold fast to" a person or thing. It can describe a garment adhering to the body (Jer 13:11), a hand gripping the hilt of a sword (2 Sam 23:10), or a tongue sticking to the roof of a parched mouth (Ps 22:15; Lam 4:4). In a relational context, it describes an active bond of steadfast loyalty between close friends or comrades (Ruth 1:14; 2 Sam 20:2; Prov 18:24) as well as a bond of romantic attraction or marital attachment between a man and a woman (Gen 2:24; 34:3; 1 Kings 11:2). The most significant use of the term appears in theological contexts, where it indicates a firm and faithful adherence to the Lord. It is the ideal human response to Yahweh expressed as love, worship, and obedience to the covenant (Deut 4:4; 10:20; 11:22; 30:20; Josh 22:5).

she has continued from early morning until now, without resting even for a moment." ᵈ

8 Then Boaz said to Ruth, "Now, listen, my daughter, do not go to glean in another field or leave this one, but keep close to my maidens. ⁹Let your eyes be upon the field which they are reaping, and go after them. Have I not charged the young men not to molest you? And when you are thirsty, go to the vessels and drink what the young men have drawn." ¹⁰Then she fell on her face, bowing to the ground, and said to him, "Why have I found favor in your eyes, that you should take notice of me, when I am a foreigner?" ¹¹But Boaz answered her, "All that you have done for your mother-in-law since the death of your husband has been fully told me, and how you left your father and mother and your native land and came to a people that you did not know before. ¹²The LORD recompense you for what you have done, and a full reward be given you by the LORD, the God of Israel, under whose wings you have come to take refuge!" ¹³Then she said, "You are most gracious to me, my lord, for you have comforted me and spoken kindly to your maidservant, though I am not one of your maidservants."

14 And at mealtime Boaz said to her, "Come here, and eat some bread, and dip your morsel in the wine." So she sat beside the reapers, and he passed to her parched grain; and she ate until she was satisfied, and she had some left over. ¹⁵When she rose to glean, Boaz instructed his young men, saying, "Let her glean even among the sheaves, and do not reproach her. ¹⁶And also pull out some from the bundles for her, and leave it for her to glean, and do not rebuke her."

17 So she gleaned in the field until evening; then she beat out what she had gleaned, and it was about an ephah of barley. ¹⁸And she took it up and went into the city; she showed her mother-in-law what she had gleaned, and she also brought out and gave her what food she had left over after being satisfied. ¹⁹And her mother-in-law said to her, "Where did you glean today? And where have you worked? Blessed be the man who took notice of you." So she told her mother-in-law with whom she had worked, and said, "The name of the man with whom I worked today is Boaz." ²⁰And Na′omi said to her daughter-in-law, "Blessed be he by the LORD, whose kindness has not forsaken the living or the dead!" Na′omi also said to her, "The man is a relative of ours, one of our nearest kin." ²¹And Ruth the Moabitess said, "Besides, he said to me, 'You shall keep close by my servants, till they have finished all my harvest.'" ²²And Na′omi said to Ruth, her daughter-in-law, "It is well, my daughter, that you go out with his maidens, lest in another field you be molested." ²³So she kept close to the maidens of Boaz, gleaning until the end of the barley and wheat harvests; and she lived with her mother-in-law.

Ruth and Boaz at the Threshing Floor

3 Then Na′omi her mother-in-law said to her, "My daughter, should I not seek a home for you, that it

---

2:8-16 Boaz shows extraordinary kindness and generosity to Ruth. He goes beyond the demands of the Mosaic Law as well as cultural expectation to ensure that she, although a displaced foreigner of low social standing, is both protected and provided for (CCC 2447). • *Allegorically*, Ruth is both a foreigner and beset with extreme poverty, yet Boaz does not despise her on either account. So too Christ accepts the Church, who is a stranger and in dire need. And just as Ruth is not allied to her companion until she leaves kin and country behind, so the Church does not become lovely to her Bridegroom until she leaves her old ways behind (St. John Chrysostom, *Homilies on Matthew* 3).

2:8 my daughter: Boaz assumes a fatherly posture toward Ruth (3:10), who is probably much younger than he, just as Naomi acts as a motherly figure toward her (2:2; 3:1).

2:9 molest: The danger is harassment or abuse, sexual or otherwise, by the field workers.

2:11 left ... your native land: Like the patriarch Abraham, who left the lands and gods of his ancestors to follow the Lord into Canaan (Gen 12:1-5; Josh 24:2-3).

2:12 full reward: The Lord responds favorably to loyalty and faith. That Boaz expects such abundant blessings for a foreigner gives witness to the universal Lordship of Yahweh. The God of Israel is the God of all nations; every person who responds to his goodness can therefore expect to receive blessings in return. • Looking forward to the NT, the words of Boaz anticipate (1) the joy that Jesus expresses when he finds genuine faith in non-Israelites (Lk 7:9) as well as (2) Peter's conviction that God accepts everyone, even Gentiles, when they fear him and do what is right (Acts 10:34-35). **wings:** Yahweh is likened to a mother bird protecting her young beneath her wings, as also in Deut 32:11; Ps 91:4; Is 31:5 (CCC 239).

2:17 ephah: More than half a bushel of grain. It represents a significant amount of work for one person to accomplish in a single day (2:7).

2:20 nearest kin: Boaz is identified in Hebrew as a *go'el* or "kinsman redeemer". This was a close relative responsible for protecting the interests of his extended family and coming to their aid in times of need. Two laws that govern his role underlie the story in Ruth. **(1)** The *redemption law* of Lev 25:25 urges a kinsman redeemer to buy back the property of a near relative who was forced to sell it because of poverty. This situation comes into play when Naomi, destitute and bereaved, prepares to sell the lands of her deceased husband, Elimelech (4:3). **(2)** The *levirate law* of Deut 25:5-6 summons an eligible brother (or, by implication, a male kinsman if no brother is living) to marry the widow of his deceased brother if the first marriage produced no children to inherit the family name and estate. This situation materializes when Naomi and Ruth are both widowed and neither has a living son (1:3-5). Boaz will fulfill this responsibility by marrying Ruth and fathering a male heir, Obed (4:13-17). For other duties incumbent upon a kinsman redeemer, see word study: *Redeem* at Lev 25:25.

2:23 until the end: The spring grain harvest lasted about two months, beginning in late April and ending in early June (1:22).

3:1-5 Naomi takes the initiative to secure a brighter future for Ruth by proposing a plan to end her poverty and widowhood. Naomi's concern for the welfare of her daughter-in-law reciprocates the devotion that Ruth has shown her in chaps. 1-2.

ᵈCompare Gk Vg: the meaning of the Hebrew text is uncertain.

may be well with you? ²Now is not Boaz our kinsman, with whose maidens you were? See, he is winnowing barley tonight at the threshing floor. ³Wash therefore and anoint yourself, and put on your best clothes and go down to the threshing floor; but do not make yourself known to the man until he has finished eating and drinking. ⁴But when he lies down, observe the place where he lies; then, go and uncover his feet and lie down; and he will tell you what to do." ⁵And she replied, "All that you say I will do."

6 So she went down to the threshing floor and did just as her mother-in-law had told her. ⁷And when Boaz had eaten and drunk, and his heart was merry, he went to lie down at the end of the heap of grain. Then she came softly, and uncovered his feet, and lay down. ⁸At midnight the man was startled, and turned over, and behold, a woman lay at his feet! ⁹He said, "Who are you?" And she answered, "I am Ruth, your maidservant; spread your garment over your maidservant, for you are next of kin." ¹⁰And he said, "May you be blessed by the LORD, my daughter; you have made this last kindness greater than the first, in that you have not gone after young men, whether poor or rich. ¹¹And now, my daughter, do not fear, I will do for you all that you ask, for all my fellow townsmen know that you are a woman of worth. ¹²And now it is true that I am a near kinsman, yet there is a kinsman nearer than I. ¹³Remain this night, and in the morning, if he will do the part of the next of kin for you, well; let him do it; but if he is not willing to do the part of the next of kin for you, then, as the LORD lives, I will do the part of the next of kin for you. Lie down until the morning."

14 So she lay at his feet until the morning, but arose before one could recognize another; and he said, "Let it not be known that the woman came to the threshing floor." ¹⁵And he said, "Bring the mantle you are wearing and hold it out." So she held it, and he measured out six measures of barley, and laid it upon her; then she went into the city. ¹⁶And when she came to her mother-in-law, she said, "How did you fare, my daughter?" Then she told her all that the man had done for her, ¹⁷saying, "These six measures of barley he gave to me, for he said, 'You must not go back empty-handed to your mother-in-law.'" ¹⁸She replied, "Wait, my daughter, until you learn how the matter turns out, for the man will not rest, but will settle the matter today."

The Marriage of Boaz and Ruth

4 And Boaz went up to the gate and sat down there; and behold, the next of kin, of whom Boaz had spoken, came by. So Boaz said, "Turn aside, friend; sit down here"; and he turned aside and sat down. ²And he took ten men of the elders of the city, and said, "Sit down here"; so they sat down. ³Then he said to the next of kin, "Na'omi, who has come back from the country of Moab, is selling the parcel of land which belonged to our kinsman Elim'elech. ⁴So I thought I would tell you of it, and say, Buy it in the presence of those sitting here, and in the presence of the elders of my people. If you will redeem it, redeem it; but if you will not, tell me, that I may know, for there is no one besides you to redeem it, and I come after you." And he said, "I will redeem it." ⁵Then Boaz said, "The day you buy the field from the hand of Na'omi, you are

---

3:2 threshing floor: A cleared platform, usually elevated and exposed to the wind, where grains were separated from their stalks and husks by a process of beating and winnowing. Farmers such as Boaz would spend the night at the threshing site in order to guard the harvest against thieves and hungry animals (3:7).

3:3 Wash ... anoint ... put on: Actions that signal the end of a period of grieving (as in 2 Sam 12:20). Ruth is not only to make herself attractive to Boaz; she is to advertise herself as a widow who is now ready to remarry. It may be that she has previously worn the distinctive clothing of a widow (cf. Gen 38:14, 19). **best clothes:** The Hebrew refers to a long over-garment that kept the poor warm at night (Ex 22:26–27).

3:4 uncover his feet: Uncovering the legs was a bold but not inappropriate way of eliciting a marriage proposal. The meaning of this symbolic gesture is not lost on Boaz (3:10–13).

3:9 spread your garment: Symbolic of the intention to marry (Ezek 16:8). Interestingly, the word translated "garment" is the same Hebrew term rendered "wings" in 2:12, hinting that Ruth will find protection in the arms of Boaz, just as she found shelter in the Lord and a place among his people.

3:10 the first: A reference to Ruth's kindness toward Naomi described in 2:11.

3:11 woman of worth: I.e., a woman of strong and noble character. For the significance of the Hebrew expression, see word study: *Good Wife* at Prov 31:10.

3:12 kinsman nearer than I: Boaz stands second in line behind a closer relative who has a prior claim to Ruth's hand in marriage. This legal obstacle to the union of Boaz and Ruth sets the stage for the events of chap. 4.

3:13 not willing: An option frowned upon but nevertheless accounted for in the Torah's levirate law (Deut 25:7). See note on 2:20. **as the LORD lives:** A traditional oath formula that attaches the sacred name of Yahweh to a solemn pledge. Boaz thereby gives Ruth the strongest assurance of his commitment to better her situation (3:11).

3:15 six measures: Exact amount uncertain, but the generosity and attentiveness of Boaz are again underscored (as in 2:8–16).

4:1–17 The story builds to suspense (4:1–7), giving way to joyful resolution (4:7–17).

4:1 the gate: The entryway into a walled settlement was the place in ancient Israel where the town council of elders made legal decisions and oversaw business transactions (Deut 25:7–10). **the next of kin ... came by:** Readers are meant to view the timing of his arrival as providential, an arrangement of the Lord to bring matters to a swift conclusion (CCC 302–3). **friend:** Better translated "so-and-so". The expression is used as a substitute for a proper noun, the name of the man being unimportant for the story. For the duty that falls to him as Naomi's closest living relative, see note on 2:20.

4:3 selling: Real estate was often sold when the landowner sank into poverty (Lev 25:25). Some scholars maintain that Naomi is not actually selling the property but offering the right to use and profit from her husband's land to an eligible kinsman.

4:4 I come after you: Boaz is next in line to exercise the rights of a kinsman redeemer. For the order in which an inheritance passes to family members, see Num 27:8–11.

4:5 buying: Or "acquiring". **widow of the dead:** Ruth is legally termed the widow of the deceased Elimelech insofar as his surviving wife, Naomi, is too elderly to bear

also buying Ruth[e] the Moabitess, the widow of the dead, in order to restore the name of the dead to his inheritance." ⁶Then the next of kin said, "I cannot redeem it for myself, lest I impair my own inheritance. Take my right of redemption yourself, for I cannot redeem it."

7 Now this was the custom in former times in Israel concerning redeeming and exchanging: to confirm a transaction, the one drew off his sandal and gave it to the other, and this was the manner of attesting in Israel. ⁸So when the next of kin said to Boaz, "Buy it for yourself," he drew off his sandal. ⁹Then Boaz said to the elders and all the people, "You are witnesses this day that I have bought from the hand of Na'omi all that belonged to Elim'elech and all that belonged to Chil'ion and to Mahlon. ¹⁰Also Ruth the Moabitess, the widow of Mahlon, I have bought to be my wife, to perpetuate the name of the dead in his inheritance, that the name of the dead may not be cut off from among his brethren and from the gate of his native place; you are witnesses this day." ¹¹Then all the people who were at the gate, and the elders, said, "We are witnesses. May the LORD make the woman, who is coming into your house, like Rachel and Leah, who together built up the house of Israel. May you prosper in Eph'rathah and be renowned in Bethlehem; ¹²and may your house be like the house of Per'ez, whom Ta'mar bore to Judah, because of the children that the LORD will give you by this young woman."

The Genealogy of David

13 So Boaz took Ruth and she became his wife; and he went in to her, and the LORD gave her conception, and she bore a son. ¹⁴Then the women said to Na'omi, "Blessed be the LORD, who has not left you this day without next of kin; and may his name be renowned in Israel! ¹⁵He shall be to you a restorer of life and a nourisher of your old age; for your daughter-in-law who loves you, who is more to you than seven sons, has borne him." ¹⁶Then Na'omi took the child and laid him in her bosom, and became his nurse. ¹⁷And the women of the neighborhood gave him a name, saying, "A son has been born to Na'omi." They named him O'bed; he was the father of Jesse, the father of David.

18 Now these are the descendants of Per'ez: Perez was the father of Hezron, ¹⁹Hezron of Ram, Ram of Ammin'adab, ²⁰Ammin'adab of Nahshon, Nahshon of Salmon, ²¹Salmon of Boaz, Boaz of O'bed, ²²O'bed of Jesse, and Jesse of David.

4:7: Deut 25:8–10.

---

children and produce a biological heir (1:12). Strictly speaking, Ruth is the widow of Elimelech's son, Mahlon (4:10). **restore the name:** A reference to Deut 25:7, where the stated purpose of levirate marriage is to propagate the family name of a deceased Israelite. **his inheritance:** Responsibility for Elimelech's land and ancestral line go together, since whatever progeny might come from Ruth would be entitled to his property.

4:6 lest I impair my own: The next of kin, motivated by self-interest, stands in contrast to Boaz, who acts in the best interest of Naomi, Ruth, and their deceased spouses.

4:7 his sandal: Removing the sandal indicates that the right of purchase is being publicly declined, and handing the sandal to another kinsman means the right is being transferred to the next relative with a claim to it. The sandal ritual in Deut 25:6–10 has a different meaning that applies to a different situation.

4:9–10 Boaz accepts the double responsibility of redeeming Elimelech's land and marrying his surviving daughter-in-law.

4:9 this day: As promised in 3:13 and anticipated in 3:18.

4:10 bought: Or "acquired".

4:11 Rachel and Leah: The two wives of the patriarch Jacob, whose sons fathered the 12 tribes of Israel (Gen 29:15–30). The prayer is that Ruth would likewise become a revered matriarch among God's people. **Ephrathah:** A clan of the tribe of Judah settled in or near Bethlehem (Mic 5:2). Boaz is presumably a member of this clan.

4:12 Perez: One of the twin sons of the patriarch Judah, born to his daughter-in-law Tamar (Gen 38:24–30). • Anticipating the circumstances of Obed's birth to Boaz and Ruth, Perez was likewise born to an Israelite father (Judah) and a widowed mother (Tamar) after another kinsman (Onan) was unwilling to accept the responsibility of fathering a child with her (as in 4:6).

4:13 he went in to her: A euphemism meaning that Boaz enters the bridal chamber to consummate his marriage with Ruth. **the LORD gave her conception:** A child is a blessing from God, who can grant or withhold the fruit of the womb (Gen 30:2; Ps 127:3; CCC 2378). It may be that Ruth is infertile, having had no children after several years of marriage (1:3–5). If so, the author is describing a miracle of divine intervention.

4:15 more ... than seven sons: An extraordinary compliment to Ruth, since having seven sons meant extraordinary blessedness (1 Sam 2:5; Job 1:2; 2 Mac 7:1).

4:16 laid him in her bosom: A tender scene of the child being received into the arms (or lap) of his grandmother. At this moment, Naomi's emptiness becomes fullness once again (1:21). Some interpret the gesture in light of an ancient adoption ritual, in which a newborn is placed on the knees of the adoptive parent. This would explain why the boy is said to belong to Naomi in the following verse, even though the infant is neither her son nor her grandson by natural descent (4:17).

4:17 Obed: His name means "one who serves". **father of Jesse ... David:** Little is known of Obed beyond the fact that he became the grandfather of the illustrious King David.

4:18–22: The genealogy of Judah spanning ten generations from Perez to David. The same names and line of descent appear also in 1 Chron 2:5–15. • Closing the book in this way makes the story of Ruth part of the larger story of salvation history. It shows that the Lord blessed the lives of Ruth, Boaz, and Naomi in order to continue the messianic line of Judah. Unknown to these figures at the time, their story was destined to have an impact on the future of Israel through the birth of King David and eventually the future of the world through the birth of the Messiah. This ultimate purpose is made clear in the opening of the Gospel of Matthew, where the same genealogy is followed from Perez to David (Mt 1:3–6) and then extended from David to Jesus Christ (Mt 1:7–16). • It is appropriate that the Lord, who came to call the Gentiles into the Church, became flesh in a family line that included Gentiles (St. Ambrose, *Exposition of Luke* 3, 33).

---

[e] Old Latin Vg: Heb *of Naomi and from Ruth.*

STUDY QUESTIONS

Chapter 1

For understanding
1. **1:1.** Who are the judges in the period before the founding of the Davidic monarchy? When in this period is the story of Ruth set? With what does the loyalty of its main characters stand in contrast? At the beginning of this story, what is ironic about the name Bethlehem? Where is Moab? Although intermarriage with Moabites was not strictly prohibited, what were Moabites forbidden to join? To what union does Scripture trace the origin of the Moabites?
2. **1:8.** What does the Hebrew word *ḥesed* denote? Why will the Lord manifest his loving concern for Ruth, and how? What, in part, is the lesson?
3. **Word study: Clung (1:14).** What does the Hebrew word *dabaq* mean? What sorts of actions can it describe? In a relational context, what does it describe? What does it indicate in theological contexts?
4. **1:16–17.** How does Ruth pledge lifelong loyalty to Naomi? In so doing, what legal and religious effects result? What does Ruth do by forsaking her home and native religion, and of what does she become a model? According to St. Paulinus of Nola, what is signified by Ruth and Orpah going their separate ways?

For application
1. **1:1–5.** Have you or your family ever been forced by necessity to move to an unfamiliar location? If so, what were some of the financial, emotional, social, and even spiritual consequences of the move for you personally and for the family?
2. **1:8–9.** To which side of your family—the maternal or paternal side—do you feel closer? If you are married, how would you characterize your relationship with your in-laws (as compared with your relationship with your own parents), and why? How does the commandment to honor one's father and mother apply to the parents of one's spouse?
3. **1:16–17.** Conversion can entail making a complete break with certain relationships and with former attitudes toward faith. Have you yourself experienced such a conversion? What sorts of breaks with the past have you made, and with what did you replace the former attachments?
4. **1:20–21.** Naomi calls herself Mara, meaning "bitter", a name that describes how she regards what God did to her in Moab. How do you regard yourself when your fortunes turn sour or disaster strikes? What questions do you ask of God under those circumstances?

Chapter 2

For understanding
1. **2:2.** What is someone who *gleans* doing? What did the Torah require landowners to do? Why?
2. **2:8–16.** What, according to the note, indicates that Boaz is going beyond the call of duty in showing kindness toward Ruth? According St. John Chrysostom, Ruth is an allegorical prefigurement of what? How are the two similar?
3. **2:12.** The Lord responds favorably to what virtues, and to what does the expectation of Boaz for blessings to a foreigner give witness? If the God of Israel is the God of all nations, what can every person who responds to his goodness expect? Looking forward to the New Testament, what do the words of Boaz anticipate? To what does the mention of wings suggest that Yahweh is likened?
4. **2:20.** What does the Hebrew word *go'el* mean? For what was this close relative responsible? What are the two laws that govern his role in the story of Ruth? How will Boaz fulfill his responsibility?

For application
1. **2:4.** Read the note for this verse. Does your relationship with the Lord carry over into your workplace? How should it do so?
2. **2:11–12.** What impresses Boaz about Ruth? What characteristics most often impress you about other people? What characteristics might impress God?
3. **2:13.** In her answer to Boaz, Ruth's language shows that she is aware of and accepts her low social status. How aware are you of your status as a creature before God? How heartfelt is your acceptance of that status? How does it influence the way you address God in prayer?
4. **2:20.** Review the note for this verse. How does the Hebrew concept of a *go'el* apply to extended family situations today? What responsibility do you have for disabled or elderly members of your own family? How willing are you to take on such a responsibility if it does not now exist?

Chapter 3

For understanding
1. **3:2.** What was a threshing floor, and how was it used? Why would farmers such as Boaz spend the night at their threshing floors?

2.   **3:3.** What are the actions of washing, anointing, and putting on her best clothes meant to signal? What is Ruth supposed to be doing? To what does the Hebrew for "best clothes" refer?
3.   **3:9.** What does the spreading of Boaz's garment symbolize? What might be suggested by the fact that the word translated "garment" here is rendered "wings" in 2:12?
4.   **3:13.** What does the oath formula "as the Lord lives" do? What does Boaz thereby give Ruth by using it?

For application
1.   **3:3–4.** (For both men and women:) How do you make yourself attractive to those whom you want to notice you for both personal and occupational reasons? Does your way of making yourself attractive accord with the virtue of modesty?
2.   **3:5–9.** What character traits does Ruth display through her behavior in these verses? What indications of romantic love for Boaz do you see in her asking him to marry her? How might the absence of romantic love (at least at this point) not be an obstacle to a happy marriage?
3.   **3:10–13.** What character traits do you see in Boaz's response? What appear to be his motives in accepting her proposal? What is his attitude toward Ruth, and how does he show it (see also v. 15)?

Chapter 4

For understanding
1.   **4:1.** What function did the entryway into a walled settlement serve in ancient Israel? How are readers meant to view the timing of the arrival of Naomi's next of kin? Why is the expression "friend" (better translated "so-and-so") used as a substitute for a man's proper noun?
2.   **4:5.** Why does Boaz refer to Ruth rather than Naomi, his surviving wife, as legally the widow of the deceased Elimelech? Of whom is Ruth the widow, strictly speaking? What is the stated purpose of levirate marriage? What does it mean that responsibility for Elimelech's land and ancestral line go together?
3.   **4:7.** What does the gesture of removing the sandal indicate? What does handing the sandal to another kinsman indicate?
4.   **4:16.** How do some interpret the gesture of Naomi placing the newborn child "in her bosom"? What would the gesture explain?
5.   **4:18–22.** What purpose does closing the book of Ruth with a genealogy of Judah spanning ten generations from Perez to David accomplish for the story? Unknown to Ruth, Boaz, and Naomi at the time, what impact would their story have on the future of Israel? How was the ultimate purpose made clear in the opening of the Gospel of Matthew?

For application
1.   **4:1.** What is "divine Providence" (see CCC 302ff.)? Have events in your own life illustrated God's Providence? Have there been some happy "coincidences" that have encouraged you to trust in God even more?
2.   **4:3–6.** Why do you think Boaz discloses only gradually what is involved in buying Elimelech's property? What are the advantages and disadvantages for both buyer and seller in handling transactions this way?
3.   **4:9–11.** What is the function of a *witness* in a transaction such as the one being narrated here? in a court trial? in an evangelistic presentation? In your personal circumstances, how are you being called to witness to your faith?
4.   **4:18–22.** How far back can you trace your ancestry? What does your ancestry tell you about yourself? What might it indicate about your family's future? Can you see the Providence of God entering into your family's history?

BOOKS OF THE BIBLE

THE OLD TESTAMENT (OT)

Gen	Genesis
Ex	Exodus
Lev	Leviticus
Num	Numbers
Deut	Deuteronomy
Josh	Joshua
Judg	Judges
Ruth	Ruth
1 Sam	1 Samuel
2 Sam	2 Samuel
1 Kings	1 Kings
2 Kings	2 Kings
1 Chron	1 Chronicles
2 Chron	2 Chronicles
Ezra	Ezra
Neh	Nehemiah
Tob	Tobit
Jud	Judith
Esther	Esther
Job	Job
Ps	Psalms
Prov	Proverbs
Eccles	Ecclesiastes
Song	Song of Solomon
Wis	Wisdom
Sir	Sirach (Ecclesiasticus)
Is	Isaiah
Jer	Jeremiah
Lam	Lamentations
Bar	Baruch
Ezek	Ezekiel
Dan	Daniel
Hos	Hosea
Joel	Joel
Amos	Amos
Obad	Obadiah
Jon	Jonah
Mic	Micah
Nahum	Nahum
Hab	Habakkuk
Zeph	Zephaniah
Hag	Haggai
Zech	Zechariah
Mal	Malachi
1 Mac	1 Maccabees
2 Mac	2 Maccabees

THE NEW TESTAMENT (NT)

Mt	Matthew
Mk	Mark
Lk	Luke
Jn	John
Acts	Acts of the Apostles
Rom	Romans
1 Cor	1 Corinthians
2 Cor	2 Corinthians
Gal	Galatians
Eph	Ephesians
Phil	Philippians
Col	Colossians
1 Thess	1 Thessalonians
2 Thess	2 Thessalonians
1 Tim	1 Timothy
2 Tim	2 Timothy
Tit	Titus
Philem	Philemon
Heb	Hebrews
Jas	James
1 Pet	1 Peter
2 Pet	2 Peter
1 Jn	1 John
2 Jn	2 John
3 Jn	3 John
Jude	Jude
Rev	Revelation (Apocalypse)

Dear Visitor

I love the gardens at Athelhampton - the way that the great vista as you approach the house gives way to a series of intimate "outdoor rooms". Everyone has their own favourite, I won't tell you mine but as a hint, it's the warmest! The gardens look wonderful even in their Winter austerity, and as the flowers burst out in Spring, the Lime Walk becomes a lovely shady tunnel, repaying all the hard work of pleaching. I love the walk alongside the River Piddle, which draws the visitor from the older gardens to the east around the house to the broad west lawn, which has its own little hidden secrets. And don't forget the kitchen garden, which may be supplying the produce for your lunch!

But above all I lov
gardens - the Martyns whose Tudor gardens are buried beneath today's lawns; the farmers whose cowsheds were here when Thomas Hardy first visited - and the extraordinary combination of Victorian eccentric Alfred Cart de Lafontaine and the man he commissioned to first lay out what we see today: the polymath Inigo Thomas. The Cooke family made improvements across three generations and now the gardens are in the charge of Sophy Davies. Her notes throughout this guide bring to life the skill and knowledge that she, Lauren Atkinson and the rest of the team use to maintain and develop the gardens for us all to enjoy.

Giles Keating

THE GARDENS AT ATHELHAMPTON

Today Athelhampton is surrounded by award-winning gardens which were created in 1891 by Mr Alfred Cart de Lafontaine who had purchased the house that year.

He was working on an ancient site. From archaeological surveys carried out during the planning of the Puddletown bypass, we know that the valley created by the River Piddle was home to numerous Iron Age settlements and the first garden at Athelhampton may date to this era. Typically, a small enclosed area of tilled soil would have been home to native species such as wild strawberries, beetroot, sorrel, mint, rosehip and celery. After the Romans arrived in AD43, they built a road from Dorchester to Salisbury that passes just 200 metres to the south of Athelhampton, which is on a sheltered and well irrigated site ideal for a villa. A Roman garden at Athelhampton would have been a formal ornamental space for pleasure with non-native plants from across the Roman empire, including box, rosemary and lavender for hedging and colourful flowers such as crocus and pansy.

By AD 850 there was a Saxon settlement at Athelhampton, which would have emphasised plants used for eating, medicine and practical crafts. The ornamental style of the Romans had largely fallen out of favour, except in some monasteries. In the Domesday book, Pydelathelhampson is shown as owned by the bishop of Salisbury, with Oldbold as his tenant. By this time, the Saxon buildings had probably been replaced by a medieval settlement, but it is unlikely that ornamental gardens had returned.

In 1485, as the Tudor dynasty began the The Great Hall was built by Sir William Martyn. While the land around Athelhampton would be used first and foremost for livestock, crops and hunting, a small formal garden would have been an important feature for the Tudor Knight.

The hammer-beam roof and stained glass in the Hall at Athelhampton are extravagant showpieces of the Martyn family wealth and a garden influenced by new ideas and styles from France and Italy would have been needed to demonstrate the family status. Formal beds contained neatly clipped woody herbs such as lavender, thyme and marjoram, and there would also be rose bushes, ponds, topiary and sundials.

The house was extended at the start of the Elizabethan era in 1558, and the gardens would have been enlarged to complement this and ensure attractive views from upper windows. Larger lawns and more symmetrical designs would likely have been added and with the introduction of cultivated flowers, the gardens would have been awash with colours rarely seen before.

Sir Robert Long, Auditor of the Exchequer to Queen Henrietta Maria, purchased Athelhampton in 1640, adding to his large land portfolio; his descendants inherited further wealth from East India Company governor Sir Josiah Child. Cultivars from the newly explored Southern states of what would become the USA were introduced to the family's houses and at Athelhampton, you can still see some of the earliest examples of Magnolia Grandiflora and Monterey Pine in England. But there was less emphasis on ornamental gardening here than at other houses where the family spent more time, notably Wanstead where Sir James Long set about creating gardens that would compare to Versailles and Villandry.

In 1848 luck ran out for William Pole-Tylney-Long-Wellesley, whose rakish lifestyle forced the sale of Athelhampton, which he had inherited from his wife Catherine Long. George Wood was the buyer and his family lived here for two generations, making it the centre of a busy farming estate.

Photographs from the 1860s show a neatly manicured lawn where the drive is now situated and large greenhouses between the Elizabethan Gable and the thatched Coach House. The rest of the land appears to be used for farming and the spoils of such activities, with pictures of cowsheds on the site of today's Green Court. Nowadays, only the Brick Colonnade and Cottage Garden remain from his time.

In 1891 a young and wealthy gentleman, Alfred Cart de Lafontaine, purchased Athelhampton with a view to restoring the manor house and creating formal gardens. The gardens were the first commission for a young architect and garden designer, Francis Inigo Thomas, who had met Alfred a few years earlier at Oxford University.

Thomas had extensively researched English garden design from the Elizabethan era onwards and took a grand tour of French and Italian gardens before starting work at Athelhampton. He drew these influences together in a way that he later described in a 1900 article, in which he argued that the three chief characteristics of old gardens were enclosure, subdivision and change of level: "As you have the dining room, library and gallery, so out of doors you have one court for guests to alight in, another for flowers and a third for the lawn game of the period."

Construction of the four formal courts required 40,000 tons of Ham Hill stone to be bought to the site. The farm buildings were cleared and the ground leveled. The progress was rapid, with the structure completed and garden planting starting in 1892.

A second phase of plans for the western side of the House was drawn up by Thomas Mawson in 1901, but for reasons unknown, these plans never proceeded.

Lafontaine would sell his beloved Athelhampton in 1918, The gardens would change little over the next 40 years with three families, Cochrane *(1919-30)*, Harmsworth *(1930-46)*, and Philips *(1949-57)* living at Athelhampton.

In 1957 Robert Victor Cooke purchased Athelhampton, and 10 years later his son Robert Cooke MP would extend the gardens further. Wild areas that bordered the formal gardens were cleared of old growth and two new ponds were added in the 1960s and 1970s, each complimenting the original plans of Inigo Thomas.

Athelhampton has shown its gardens to the public since 1911, with weekend opening between the world wars. In 1963 the Cooke family opened the gardens to the public on a regular basis, the income supporting the work of the gardening team. The historic interest of the gardens was identified in 1986 when they were added to the National Heritage List for England as Grade 1. The work of the Cooke family was recognised with the 1997 Garden of the year award.

The Cooke family sold Athelhampton to Giles Keating in 2019 and the team continue to work hard to maintain and protect these historic award-winning gardens for generations to come.

William North, Head Gardener, 1899

GREAT COURT

The Great Court is the largest court garden at Athelhampton, and is considered to be Francis Inigo Thomas' masterpiece. Originally laid out as a Parterre with beds punctuated with yew trees at their corners, in the 1890s it contained wild flowers, and by the 1930s rose bushes.

At the end of the second world war, Athelhampton's owner Mrs Harmsworth married Sir John Blunt and subsequently moved away. The house and gardens were left to decay, and in few years, the Parterre disappeared. Today, 130 years later after their first planting the yew pyramids dominate the garden.

The 1972 movie 'Sleuth' was filmed on the sunken lawn, with a maze constructed temporarily for filming. At the beginning of the film the character Milo Tindle *(Michael Caine)* has to navigate through the maze to reach Andrew Wyke *(Sir Laurence Olivier)*. Both men would be nominated for Best Actor at the Academy Awards.

In the 1970s two flower beds beneath the terrace were turned into long lily ponds, and later into bog gardens. We have plans to restore these ponds in the next few years.

Head Gardener's notes –
*Over the past 130 years our topiary **Taxus baccata** (Yew) pyramids have outgrown the original design that Francis Inigo Thomas created for the Great Court. Since Alfred Cart de Lafontaine left Athelhampton all twelve Yew trees have been allowed to grow and consume the space where the traditional English parterre garden once was. Despite their enormous size, grand old age and yearly clipping the yew pyramids continue to flower and thrive.*

The Parterre, 1899

Michael Caine & Lawrence Olivier, 1971

THE TERRACE

The Terrace, with its balustrade and tapering staircase is constructed from Ham stone and lies at the south of The Great Court. The Terrace offers a wide view over Athelhampton, including the Coach House, the Colonnade, the medieval Dovecote, the West Wing and Great Hall of the Tudor Manor. From the centre point of the terrace you can view the main axis of the garden, through the Corona and Green Court, with fountains in each.

Early designs for the terrace show hidden potting sheds beneath the paved area, but these were never realised, however the two garden pavilions that were part of that design remain. To the west is the House of Joy and Summer, with a carved face smiling down above the door. The eastern house is the House of Sorrow and Winter, with a tortured face and icicles.

The attics of each pavilion contain huge tanks, designed to be filled with water from a steam powered pump. Once full, the water could be released at the turn of the tap to feed all the ponds and fountains by gravity. The tanks are still in situ, but not used, instead we use electricity generated by our solar panels to run an energy efficient pump.

Head Gardener's notes –
*Although planting in the shadows of such large topiary is an ongoing challenge, the 'bog' gardens below the terrace walls continue to flourish. With jurassic sized **Gunnera manicata** leaves, troublemaking **Equisetum arvense** (Mare's tail) and delicate white **Zantedeschia aethiopica** (Calla/Arum Lily) all contained within the old lead pond liners, this garden comes alive with lush green growth and floral statements.*

The Bog Gardens, 2020

Garden of the Year Award, 1997

THE CORONA

The Corona is in the Elizabethan manner, with twenty four Ham stone obelisks raised on the scalloped wall. Francis Inigo Thomas said "The Corona is the central pivot of the Gardens". The garden was designed to give access to all the formal gardens, to the south the Great Court, to the north the Green Court, and to the east the Lion's Mouth garden.

A background of neatly clipped yew gives emphasis to the golden yellow hue of the Ham stone, beneath the walls four raised beds contain a scheme of planting little altered in over a century. At the centre of the garden a lead vase, in the manner of William Kent, punctuates the small pond. On a peaceful day the circular walls, like the whispering gallery of St Paul's Cathedral, will allow a quiet voice to be projected to a listener stood on the other side of the garden.

Head Gardener's notes -
*The beds that surround you in The Corona Garden are bursting full with maroon and deep purple herbaceous perennials. During the early weeks of spring potent purple **Hyacinthus orientalis 'Woodstock'** (Hyacinth) fill the garden with an unmistakable fragrance, shortly followed by abundant displays of majestic maroon flowers from the Dahlia **'Arabian Night'**. Although all four beds consist of identical planting schemes we continuously struggle to balance the garden as each bed, facing different directions, gets an unequal amount of sunlight. The acidity of the soil is also affected on one side by needles falling from the Cedar of Lebanon and mulching the beds. This affects the colour and quality of the summer florals. As this garden is hugged by the warm ham stone walls that surround it we are able to overwinter our Dahlia tubers in situ by adding a thick layer of compost onto each bed. Overwintering tubers in situ has great benefits to the Dahlias as well as saving us a job, the greatest benefit is avoiding the inevitable damage done to the tubers when lifting with a garden fork.*

The Corona, 1906

The Corona, 1912

LION'S MOUTH

East of the Corona lies the Lion's Mouth with its cascade and pool. This was designed as a rose garden, with raised grass banks either side of the pathway. For reasons unknown to us the roses did not thrive here, and during the 1930s they were moved to the Great Court,

In 1977 the garden was further altered to create a home for rock plants and others requiring a dry situation, with a number of gifts from the Abbey Gardens on the island of Tresco in the Scillies. These plants have thrived, with the eucalyptus and palms now reaching maturity.

A further underplanting scheme was carried out in 2019, we chose plants that would be able to enjoy the warmer dryer summers we have been experiencing, and the garden was finished with a gravel topping on the beds to provide better drainage during heavy rainfall.

Head Gardener's notes –
Although the Lion's Mouth is full of impressive 'hot climate' plants, including our well established **Phormium tenax** *(New Zealand Flax), spikey green Yukka and the stunning* **Cercis siliquastrum** *(Judas tree), the focal point of this garden is the spectacular Eucalyptus tree. At only 45 to 50 years old, this* **Eucalyptus globulus** *(Blue gum) is in a competitive spot for the tallest tree in the formal gardens. Having overtaken the Cedar of Lebanon over a decade ago it continues to climb and is now close to the hight of the* **Pinus radiata** *(Monterey Pine) planted in 1780. The Eucalyptus has an interesting life cycle as its leaf fall happens in the early summer instead of the autumn. This is key to its survival in harsher environments, however it does mean that the gardening team and I are clearing leaves all year round.*

The Lion's Mouth, 1906

The Lion's Mouth, 2022

SOUTH WALK

In 1892 as the construction of the gardens was completed, a network of gravel paths was established that would allow Alfred Cart de Lafontaine, his family, friends and later owners to enjoy a walk around the gardens and wider estate.

The path in The South Walk has long disappeared, probably during a period of decline towards the end of the Second World War when Mrs Harmsworth had re-married and moved away. Athelhampton was left with reduced care until Rodney & Marika Philips purchased Athelhampton in 1949. Today the gravel has been replaced by a grass path, giving a more natural feel to the garden.

The planting here had reached its maturity by 2020 and it was decided to replace the underplanting of the garden with a refreshed design, retaining the mature trees.

Head Gardener's notes -
*Inspired by Gertrude Jekyll, a key figure of the 'Arts and Crafts' movement in gardens, we have recently undertaken the task of replanting and reinvigorating a similarly inspired design that was planted here 20 years ago. Jekyll was a believer that patience was key to a good garden, allowing new perennial plants the time and space required to reach their potential. The newly planted borders consist of traditional cottage garden plants whilst also incorporating more drought tolerant plants as the summers become hotter and longer than ever before. Enchanting **Persicaria bistorta 'Superba'** (Persicaria) creates clusters of cylindrical pink flowers on tall stems, the proud pinnacles of Lupins, Foxglove and Delphiniums in shades of pink and blue make gentle statements whilst the shocking hot pink **Echinacea purpurea** act as bold exclamation marks in the planting.*

George Cochrane, The South Walk, 1920

The South Walk, 2020

LIME WALK

Alongside the The South Walk is the Lime Walk which is the first part of the garden in this book that was not designed by Francis Inigo Thomas.

The double row of pollarded lime trees gives the garden a natural pergola, which on a hot day shades the visitor with its large bright green leaves, and in the winter reveals the bare structure of entwined branches.

From the southerly end of the lime walk there is a view that leads the eye along the gravel path to the kitchen garden toward the River Piddle at the far end.

Head Gardener's notes –
Each garden comes with the need for its own unique set of skills, over the years I have had to acquire the skill of pleaching our **Tilia platyphyllos** *(Lime tree). Starting just before Christmas and finishing in early March, we spend hours, days, weeks and months intricately weaving in new growth to maintain this impressive canopy. Accessing such heights and angles has always been tricky, but with each year that passes we learn new ways of getting the job done. Every summer, as we work in the lime walk's shade, we are rewarded for our efforts and retire from the heat of the sun whilst admiring the delicate bright blue flowers of the* **Buglossoides purpurocaerulea** *(Purple Gromwell).*

Leaf Clearing, The Lime Walk, 2023

The Lime Walk, Winter 2015

CANAL POND

The Canal Pond was built in 1969 by Sir Robert Cooke, the then owner of Athelhampton. This long pond is created in the 17th Century manner and is the largest of the ponds at Athelhampton. It runs parallel to the Kitchen Garden and is perfectly aligned on one of the axis that Francis Inigo Thomas designed his garden around.

Beyond the fountain is the Tyneham Arch, once a doorway to a fine Elizabethan Manor. In the Second World War the nearby Dorset village of Tyneham, including the Manor, was requisitioned by the War Office for training. After the war the village was retained by the War Office, the Manor house was neglected and within a few years was falling apart, and by the 1960s had been demolished, a handful of architectural items were saved by local landowners.

Head Gardener's notes -
*The Canal pond is home to a few of the many **Magnolia grandiflora** we have at Athelhampton. However a more interesting specimen of Magnolia has been growing here, over the doorway into the Kitchen Garden, since long before the Canal pond was built. **Magnolia delavayi** is described as one of the most spectacular Chinese evergreen Magnolias and is without doubt one of my favourite plants in the gardens. It is visibly unique with its large crinkly blue-green leaves, whilst at the same time it tips its hat to the grandiflora with a beautiful display of large white flowers in the summer.*

Gyb the Cat, The Canal Pond, 2021

The Canal Pond, 1995

KITCHEN GARDEN

The one acre Kitchen Garden at Athelhampton was created by Alfred Cart de Lafontaine following plans drawn up by the Garden Designer Thomas Mawson. The high walls are in contrast to the other gardens with Ham stone replaced by London brick, perhaps an indication that this garden was designed with function in mind, as the walls protect the garden from predators and the elements, and they also establish an inner micro-climate, with the retained heat encouraging fruit and vegetables to grow in abundance.

With the reduction of servants, domestic staff and those reliant on Athelhampton during the 1950s the need for such a large amount of food production declined and the garden was unused. A scheme to restore the garden in the 1970s was delayed until 2014 when Patrick and Andrea Cooke started a restoration that would take a decade.

The garden is divided into quadrants with brick paths leading to the central dipping pond, designed for filling water cans, in the centre of the pond a pillar sun-dial, with four faces and gnomons which tell the time from dawn to dusk.

Head Gardener's notes -
*From the Mange tout in the vegetable beds to the **Knautia macedonica** in the herbaceous borders, everything growing in the Kitchen Garden must have purpose. This delicate eco-system consists of attracting pollinators, producing fruit and vegetables and feeding the soil. One favourite for this garden is **Calendula officinalis**, it is brilliant for co-planting with any fruit and vegetables as its sticky dewy foliage works perfectly at trapping pests.*

Gyb the Cat, The Kitchen Garden, 2022

"Time Flies", Sundial, The Kitchen Garden, 2022

BELL GATE

As the Lime Walk ends, the path leads on to the Kitchen Garden, or into the Green Court. The Bell Gate stands at the end of a short path, the Ham Stone gateway part of the formal garden is marked with a stylistic L on a shield, no doubt for "Lafontaine" as the iron gate confirms the date of 1891, neatly punched out of metal, the year the gardens were created.

The gate contains six brass bells, hence its name, perhaps they would once have sounded the arrival of a visitor as a driveway used to run past here. The drive has long gone, and the bells are now silent.

The path and gateway lie on one of Francis Inigo Thomas axes. Today if you stand on the path you will see the fountain in the Green Court lines up neatly with the gate, and porch door of the house, and then when you turn to face the other way, the Tyneham Arch and Canal Pond join the same line.

Head Gardener's notes –

*Under the shade of the beautiful avenue of Acacia trees, lollipops of **Alliums 'purple sensation'** grow tall sheltered from the wind, flowering in late spring through to early summer. To extend the colour in these beds a new planting of Tulip 'Negrita' provides an earlier display of purple, with their resplendent flowers lining the avenue. If you're visiting us in the later months of summer you may have missed this display, however the hues of purple are only a nod to the beautiful colour theme in the next garden as you head past the Bell Gate.*

L for Lafontaine, The Bell Gate, 2018

The Bell Gate, 1970

GREEN COURT

The Great Court with its Terrace, and the Corona are both visibly large construction works, yet the Green Court was the most complex garden to create. Athelhampton had been for many centuries a divided house, and this garden lies on one such physical divide where once an East Wing of the house, barns and other outbuildings stood.

The dividing wall and buildings were removed and the ground was cleared, presenting Cart de Lafontaine with an opportunity to create a lawn within a lawn, with a Ham stone kerb and a central pond.The design ofthe pondhas cusps ateach end exactlyreplicatingthe structure ofthe Great Hall roof. To give symmetry to the East Front of the House, a second crenelated turret was created to match the original Tudor building, both are examples of the careful design by Inigo Thomas.

Head Gardener's notes -
*Yellow **Scabiosa ochroleuca** (Scabious) and **Foeniculum vulgare** (Fennel) grow in front of the deep purple backdrop of **Cotinus coggygria** (Smoke Bush), embodying the original contrasting colour scheme of purple and yellow in this historic garden. Along the terrace, at the foot of the garden, another example of the same clever colour palette can be witnessed. A delicate yellow rose entangles the well established wisteria that leans on the stonework, combining the yellow and purple florals in a short lived but magnificent display during the later months of spring. Although this garden is largely structured with mature shrubs such as **Philadelphus coronarius**, there are still many flowers to be enjoyed. T he **Philadelphus** itself has beautiful petite white blossoms, the large Tree Peonies either side of the Corona gateway produce vibrant yellow fragrant flowers and the **Crinodendron hookerianum** (Chilean lantern tree) under the Cedar of Lebanon have unusual pendulous red blooms.*

The Green Court, 1906

Outside the scullery, 1862

ROSE GARDEN

Beyond the Green Court lies an area designed as part of the original design, but heavily altered over the years. The gardens here used wooden trellis and yew hedging rather than a physical structure and over the years most was lost to trees that matured over the following decades.

Most of the trees here were severely damaged during the Great Storm on the night of 15th October 1987. The hurricane is reported to have been famously dismissed in a weather forecast by Michael Fish on the BBC that evening. Though usually omitted from TV repeats, he did go on to say it would be 'very windy' and the hurricane would track further south than the English Channel.

The garden was cleared of fallen trees, and over the next few years the ground was prepared for a new rose garden, something that had been lacking at Athelhampton since the late 1940s.

Head Gardener's notes -
*The roses you see today are many of the originals bought for this garden. Layers of dark pink, light pink, white and yellow surround the pathways in a semi circle of fragrant florals. Although many of the names have been lost amongst the vast garden archive, a faded label was found amongst the soil when planting the box hedging. The label reads **"David Austin. Princess Alexandra of Kent"** which upon research, matches the inner layer of dark pink Roses. It is therefore fair to assume that all four colours of rose will be varieties from David Austin and on this assumption I plan to identify the remaining roses as this will be pertinent to their care and the overall upkeep of this garden. If you are visiting us in the summer months, you may notice the upper layers of foliage are beginning to curl. This is due to rose leaf-rolling sawfly which has been commonly mistaken for drought and deficiencies for several years. Sawfly are often less harmful than these common issues as they only use the plant as a host for their larvae which can be easily dealt with by using a mild horticultural soap.*

The Rose Garden, Winter 2022

The Rose Garden, Spring 2021

WHITE GARDEN

The White Garden was built in 1964 by the then owner of Athelhampton, Robert Victor Cooke FRCS in memory of his wife Elizabeth. They had purchased the house and its gardens in 1957, and their family would own Athelhampton for two further generations.

In 2022 the planting had matured in the central bed, and this garden was scheduled for re-planting, with a similar scheme, but there were concerns that air-source heat-pumps installed nearby as part of the "Athelhampton Zero" project could produce background noise that would spoil the tranquility of the garden

A decision was taken to add another pond and fountain to the garden, a lead vase would be retained as the centre piece surrounded by a short box hedge within the central bed. The sound of water gently trickling down would disguise any noise from the heat pumps.

Head Gardener's notes -
You may notice a difference when comparing the today's White Garden to the photograph opposite. Since the early Autumn of 2022, we have been working hard to create a pond in the central brick planter to bring this secluded corder of the garden to life. Above you stand two large bay trees, casting their huge shadow over the garden, making this quite a dark corner. The planting in this garden has been white for a number of years, bringing much a needed brightness into the garden. We will continue to plant this garden with white floras to maintain the bright aspect of this shady garden and to honour its service as a memorial garden.

The White Garden, Spring 2022

Memorial to Elizabeth Mary Cooke. 1964

OCTAGONAL POND

To link the White Garden to the Kitchen Garden and to compose the space between, an octagonal cloister garden was constructed in 1971/72. The layout of an octagonal pond surrounded by pleached lime trees with a central fountain was designed by Sir Robert Cooke MP, who had designed a similar scheme for New Palace Yard at the Palace of Westminster.

An inscription in the Ham Stone pond surround reads BENEDICITE CETE ET OMNIA QUAE MOVENTURE IN AQUIS DOMINO, meaning "O ye whales and all that move in the waters bless ye The Lord". The stone Pinnacle was built partly from stone recovered from a Westminster Hall buttress during repairs in the 1970s. Some new stone was used to finish the construction, but left uncarved so the original stone can be seen.

Head Gardener's notes -
*The pleached **Tilia platyphyllos** (Limes) follow the shape of the pond and provide a shaded canopy from which you can admire the pond. If you stand still in the summer you might just be lucky enough to see a giant pondhawk dragonfly take a drink from the **Nymphaea alba** (White Water-Lily). Here the water-lily flowers and leaves have a very important role in the lifecycle of the Amphibian wildlife residing in the gardens; their huge round leaves and beautiful white flowers act as nature's steps for this season's emerging froglets to leave the water and seek shelter from predators. The ponds at Athelhampton are all river fed, therefore being full of natural chalk stream wildlife as well as important and beneficial organisms. Due to increasing summer heat the blanket weed is growing faster than ever before and despite our best efforts to remove it whilst conserving wildlife some ponds may be clearer than others. Often, in early spring when the tadpoles are sheltering within the blanket weed, we may leave some ponds until the froglets emerge.*

White Lilies, 2020

Octagonal Pond during construction, 1972

THE RIVER PIDDLE

The River Piddle creates a natural boundary to the gardens at Athelhampton. The river rises on the Dorset Downs just north of the Church at Alton Pancras, before flowing southward along the Piddle Valley through villages that carry its name, Piddletrenthide, Piddlehinton, Puddletown, Tolpuddle, Affpuddle, Briantspuddle and Turnerspuddle. In the 1290s Henry Pydel owned the manor at Athelhampton, or as it was known centuries ago, Pydeleathalamston.

The water meadows beyond the river became the key to post-medieval husbandry, a network of ancient ditches, dikes and sluices that were designed for flooding and irrigation. The winter flood would prevent harsh frosts killing the grass, giving a lush spring growth.

Head Gardener's notes -
The River Piddle is a beautiful and important chalk stream. Many trout and eels swim amongst the **Ranunculus fluitans** *(Water-crowfoot). Other than putting waders on to clear a path for water flow during the summer and maintaining the man-made structures such as the weirs, sluices and culverts, we allow the river to maintain itself. It is vital to the wildlife that we don't interfere too much as we could disrupt duck and moor hen nests as well as other important breeding and feeding cycles. As the ponds are fed directly from the river you may notice the same pollinators and beneficial insects which you saw earlier in the gardens. This is the joy of naturally fed ponds and is vital to the success of the Kitchen Garden. The beauty in the natural lifecycle of the river is something we are extremely fortunate to witness and we hope that you may also enjoy the beautiful wildlife that the River Piddle brings to the gardens.*

The River Piddle, 1920

The River Piddle, 2009

WEST LAWN & DOVECOTE

The lawn is a large multiple purpose space, the families that have owned Athelhampton have played games and sports, and hosted village fetes, outdoor theatre and more recently it has become an outdoor home to members of The Royal Ballet who perform here for charity.

The lawn provides a fabulous view of the house, with the Portland Stone North Wing, built by owners George and Mary Cochrane, a glimpse through the courtyard to the East Wing, then onto the Great Hall, and the Elizabethan West Wing.

Standing beside the house is the medieval Dovecote. Inside there are niches in the stonework to provide 1500 nests. There are usually around 400 doves who come and go as they please. Around the ancient stonework is a selection of old rambling roses, the varieties unknown.

Head Gardener's notes -
Our West Lawn has some beautiful trees that enjoy the nutrient rich soil fed by the River Piddle. The two giant **Metasequoia glyptostroboides** *(Dawn Redwoods) tower high above the house creating a beautiful shaded area where a carpet of crocus splashes colour around the base of the two trees in early spring. Nearer the dovecote is an ancient Mulberry tree being propped up by a metal support bar having partly fallen in a storm many years ago, it is thought to be hundreds of years old and still produces an abundance of delicious mulberries that are perfect for jam making. There is another living thing that enjoys out nutrient rich soils on the West Lawn: moles! We are constantly battling moles coming into the formal gardens and stopping them in such a large area is nearly impossible.*

The Dovecote, 1920

The Doves on the West Wing roof, 1920